James A. Garfield
20th President of the United States

Fern G. Brown

 GARRETT EDUCATIONAL CORPORATION

Manufactured in the United States of America

Edited and produced by Synthegraphics Corporation

Library of Congress Cataloging in Publication Data

Brown, Fern G.
  James A. Garfield, 20th President of the United States / Fern G. Brown.
      p.   cm. — (Presidents of the United States)
  Includes bibliographical references.
  Summary: Presents the life of James A. Garfield, including his childhood, education, employment, and political career.
    1. Garfield, James A. (James Abram), 1831–1881 — Juvenile literature.   2. Presidents — United States — Biography — Juvenile literature.   3. United States — Politics and government — 1877–1881 — Juvenile literature.   [1. Garfield, James A. (James Abram), 1831–1881.   2. Presidents.]   I. Title II. Series.
E687.B875   1990
973.8'4'092 — dc20
[B]
[92]   89-39953
ISBN 0-944483-63-1   CIP
                                                                          AC

Contents

Chronology for
James A. Garfield

1831   Born on November 19

1848   Worked on a canal boat

1849– Attended Geauga Seminary and Western
1852   Reserve Eclectic Institute; also taught school

1853   Preached in area churches

1854– Attended Williams College
1856

1856– Professor at and president of the Eclectic
1859   Institute

1858   Married Lucretia Rudolph on November 11

1859   Elected to Ohio state senate

1861   Admitted to Ohio bar

1861– Commissioned a lieutenant colonel in Ohio
1863   Volunteer Infantry during the Civil War;
           promoted to colonel, brigadier general,
           then major general

1863– Served in the U.S. House of Representa-
1880   tives

1880   Elected to the U.S. Senate and as 20th
           President of the United States

1881   Shot on July 2 by a disappointed office
           seeker; died from wound on September 19

Chapter 1

Destined for Greatness

Charles Julius Guiteau fingered the pistol in his pocket. It was ten minutes after nine, the morning of July 2, 1881. He had just arrived at the Baltimore and Potomac Railroad Depot on 6th Street in Washington, D.C. At last he would meet up with James A. Garfield, the man who had caused all the trouble for the Republican Party — the man who had refused to appoint him to a post in the new government. He had been stalking Garfield for almost a month, and now he was going to kill the President of the United States.

Guiteau had his boots shined and entered the depot. He went directly into the bathroom and loaded his revolver. Then, he left a paper at the newsstand explaining why he was going to shoot President Garfield and sat down in the ladies' waiting room.

Ten minutes went by. President Garfield's carriage drove up to the station. Inside, Garfield was deep in conversation with Secretary of State James G. Blaine. A guard held the door for the President.

"How much time do we have?" Garfield asked.

"About ten minutes, sir," the officer answered, showing his watch.

The men in the carriage kept talking for a few more

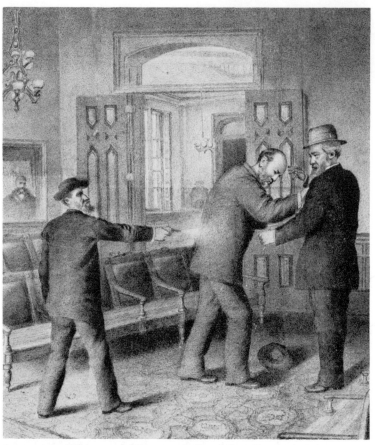

Scene at the Baltimore and Potomac Railroad Station in
Washington, D.C., on Saturday July 2, 1881. At 9:20 A.M., as
President Garfield and Secretary of State Blaine walked
through the ladies' waiting room, Charles Guiteau came up behind the President and fired two shots at him with his ivory-
handled revolver. (Library of Congress.)

minutes. Then the President stepped out and, taking Blaine's
arm, entered the ladies' waiting room where Guiteau was
lurking.

The President and secretary began to cross the room toward the main waiting room. They had gone about two-thirds
of the way when Guiteau crept up behind them, pulled out
his revolver, and fired. The shot struck Garfield in the left

shoulder. He cried out, "My God, what was that?" Another shot quickly followed, and this time the President was struck in the back, at the lower edge of the rib cage, and the bullet smashed into his abdomen. Dazed, he fell to the floor. James Abram Garfield, the 20th President of the United States, after only four months in office had been struck down by an assassin's bullet!

ANCESTORS AND EARLY LIFE

Edward Garfield, James A. Garfield's earliest known ancestor, settled in Massachusetts in 1630. After the Revolutionary War, Solomon Garfield, one of Edward's descendants, moved to Worcester, New York. It was there, three days before the dawn of the 19th century, that Solomon's grandson Abram was born. Abram was James A. Garfield's father.

Eliza Ballou, James' mother, was raised on a farm near Richmond, New Hampshire. After her father died, the Ballou family moved to Worcester, New York, where they met the Garfields. Abram Garfield, who was then 14 years old, fell in love with Eliza's sister Mehitabel (Hitty) and was very unhappy when the Ballous left Worcester for Muskingum County, Ohio. But Hitty promised to wait for marriage until Abram was old enough to come for her.

When he was 17, Abram started out for Ohio to claim his bride. But he turned back after meeting a friend on the way who told him that Hitty was already married. However, because so many of his family and friends were moving West, Abram finally went anyway. Three years later, in 1819, he arrived in Muskingum County.

The first thing Abram did was call on an uncle of the Ballous whom he had known back in New York. He stopped to ask directions from a neighbor, who later laughingly teased

Eliza that he had met the man who would be her husband. Eliza, a small, quick, popular young woman of 18, was then living with her uncle. She scoffed and said she remembered Abram as a "green boy" and had never liked him. But when she saw that Abram had grown to be a tall, handsome, broad-shouldered young man, she changed her mind about him. Within three months (February 1820), true to the neighbor's prophesy, Abram and Eliza were married. A short time later they went to live in Cuyahoga County, located in the Western Reserve (a strip of land bordering Lake Erie, in Ohio). In those days it was virtually a wilderness, but it is now the city of Cleveland.

Humble Beginnings

For the first eight years of their marriage, the Garfields did not have a home of their own. They lived off and on in Newburgh, Ohio, and Abram hired out as a farm worker. Because he was so strong, Eliza boasted that her husband did the work of two men.

The young couple worked hard under primitive conditions, often lacking the necessities of life. Eliza later wrote, "We was sick every fall regular." Yet despite sickness and poverty, the family grew. During this time, four children were born: Mehitabel (called Hitty after Eliza's sister), Thomas, Mary, and James Ballou. Because he needed money to support his growing family, Abram gave up farming and contracted to build a section of the Ohio and Erie Canal, a waterway planned to join Lake Erie with the Ohio River.

At first Abram's work was successful. Then came bad times and the business failed. But before his canal venture collapsed, Abram bought a parcel of land in Orange Township, Cuyahoga County, Ohio. While Eliza and the children remained in Newburgh, he began to build a log cabin in Orange Township for his family.

The Garfields were looking forward to moving into their own home when their youngest child, two-year-old Jimmy, suddenly became sick and died. Because they had not been very religious, Eliza and Abram thought God had punished them by taking their son. Determined to mend their godless ways and find comfort through prayer and preaching, they heard about a new religion. It was called by various names – Disciples of Christ, Christians, or Campbellites, after its founder, Alexander Campbell. The Garfields were among the many converts that the Disciples (as they called themselves) gathered in the townships of the Reserve.

LIFE ON THE RESERVE

When the Garfields moved into their new home, Eliza prayed for another son. Her prayers were answered when James Abram Garfield was born on November 19, 1831. His mother later wrote that she knew immediately that "this was a child of high destiny, born to be great and good."

When James was 18 months old, a fire broke out in the woods and Abram fought it all day long. He was exhausted, caught a chill, and shortly thereafter died of pneumonia at the age of 33.

It was the custom of the time for a young widow to sell her land and live with relatives who would care for her children while she went to work. The older children would be "put out" as helpers on farms. But Eliza Garfield chose instead to stay on her farm with her children. She sold part of the land and farmed the remaining 30 acres with the help of relatives.

Everyone in the Garfield household had to work hard in order to survive. Thomas, who was almost 12, worked in the fields. Mary and Hitty did household chores, and Mrs. Garfield took in neighbors' sewing. The children were brought up in the faith of the Disciples and, although fatherless, theirs was a loving, song-filled home.

Because Thomas had to work to help support the family, he did not attend school. His mother taught him to read from the Bible. She also taught him how to write and do simple arithmetic. Baby James, on the other hand, the bright little boy who resembled his father, became the spoiled pet of the family. When he was only three years old, his sister Hitty carried him to the district school at Chagrin Falls, three miles away. It wasn't long before he, too, was reading from the Bible.

Because Chagrin Falls was too far for James to walk every day, Mrs. Garfield persuaded her neighbors to build a schoolhouse on her land. Eliza loved all her children and did not mean to favor James. Yet in her opinion, it was not necessary for girls to go to school, and Thomas already had all the schooling he needed in order to be a farmer. But James, the bright one, had to be educated. He was destined for greatness.

A Troubled Youngster

James won a prize for reading in his first year of school. Because there were so few books, he read and reread *Robinson Crusoe* and Goodrich's *History of the United States.* Although he did well in school, James did not get along with the neighborhood boys. When they taunted him about being poor and having no father, he would run home crying to his older brother. Wanting and needing a father seemed to be a big factor in the emotional disturbances which James began to show in childhood. Other factors were his mother's obsession with the notion that illness and death were always hovering over them. Furthermore, she was continually telling her youngest son that he was destined for greatness.

James began to have ailments. The worst were blinding

headaches and severe chest and throat infections. Boils and rheumatic pains cursed him throughout his life. He was constantly worried about his digestive system, which gave him trouble whenever he was under stress. While convalescing from his frequent illnesses, James would read a great deal. His favorite books were stories of the sea, and he began to dream of going to faraway places on a sailing ship.

Mrs. Garfield's second marriage may also have contributed to James' problems. Although the exact facts are not known, the records of Cuyahoga County confirm that Eliza was married to Alfred (Warren) Belden (or Belding) on April 16, 1842, when James was 10 years old. She and James lived with Belden for about a year in Bedford, Ohio, and then went back to Orange. Because she would not return to Bedford, Belden sued for divorce.

Although Eliza tried to ignore the proceedings, she and Belden were finally divorced in 1850. In those days divorce was considered a terrible scandal. Because Eliza did not want her reputation ruined, she pretended the divorce had never happened. However, the situation seemed to affect James greatly. Years later, when he heard that his stepfather had died, he wrote in his diary, "After this long, long silence ended in death, it is hard for me to think of the man without indignation."

Becoming a Man

When James was 12 years old, he worked for neighbors after school. He made five cents a day for helping with planting and harvesting. But because he was rather clumsy, he had many accidents. Twice he struck his foot with an ax so severely that he could not work for six weeks. When he was 15 years old, James earned 50 cents a day working and living at a nearby farm for a month. However, at an age when most country boys were quite independent, he was homesick for his mother.

Besides regular school, James attended singing school and occasionally a spelling school. Sometimes he would go hunting with his friend, Orrin Judd. Other times he would help Thomas on their farm, hoeing corn or raking hay, but mostly he worked away from home to earn money.

The summer James was 16 he boarded at an uncle's farm and did very hard work. He had to cut 100 cords of wooden logs into four-foot lengths (each cord was eight feet long and four feet high). The job took James all of June and July and part of August. When he had finished and was heading home, he felt quite satisfied. He had not hurt himself once, and the 25 dollars in his pocket proved he was a man. But James did not want to chop wood all his life. He desperately longed to go to sea and become a sailor.

After walking the 15 miles from his uncle's farm, James arrived home dusty and tired. He turned all but five dollars of his money over to his mother, then he announced that he was leaving in the morning for Cleveland to become a sailor. His mother and brother tried to talk him out of it. They told him that life on the sea would be too rough and dangerous. James replied that he was a man now and could take care of himself. His mother agreed that he was big and strong and knew how to fight, but he had no experience in the ways of the world. James would not listen. His mind was made up.

CANAL BOY

The next morning, James left home to become a sailor. When he arrived at Cleveland harbor, it was crowded with sailing ships and steamers. Feeling light-hearted, James headed straight for the first ship he saw and bounded up the gang-plank. He found the captain and politely asked to be taken on as a sailor. The captain, a large, dirty man, was very drunk. He turned on the tall, blond, muscular country boy, cursed him, and told him in vile language what he thought of sea-struck adolescents. James was so upset that he quickly ran off the ship amid the jeers and raucous laughter of the deck hands.

Although he was hurt and disappointed, James was de-termined not to give up. He realized that he might not be ready to become "a real sailor" yet, but there was plenty of work on the Ohio and Erie Canal. His cousin, Amos Letcher, was captain of a canal boat, the *Evening Star.* He decided to look for his cousin on the canal.

That very night, August 16, 1848, James signed on with Captain Letcher as a driver for 12 dollars a month and his keep. "As canaling was at the bottom of sailing," James remarked later, "so driving was at the bottom of canaling." His job was to prod the horses that pulled the boat through the water. Switch in hand, he would walk along the towpath, and occasionally he would swat the horses across their rumps. It was probably just as dull a job as chopping wood, but to James, because he was working on the canal, it was exciting.

The *Evening Star* was bound for Pittsburgh with a load of copper ore. After traveling the canal by horsepower, the boat was towed by steamboat up the Ohio River. James fell overboard many times, and because he couldn't swim, his mates had to fish him out. Nevertheless, he was a good worker, and after the first trip to Pittsburgh he was promoted to bowman with a salary of 14 dollars a month. James was at ease with the rough canal men. He had earned their re-spect with his fists when he knocked down a man who chal-lenged him to a fight.

This drawing is from an old woodcut. It shows Garfield as a boy working on the canal. Garfield walked along the towpath or rode mules or dray horses and prodded the animals to move along while they pulled the barges. (Library of Congress.)

Plagued by Illness

James Garfield may have been a sailor all his life except that he fell ill after his fourth trip to Pittsburgh. He had been promoted again and his wages raised to 20 dollars a month, but he was too sick with "fever and ague" (probably malaria) to work. So Captain Letcher sent James home to be nursed back to health by his mother.

James' illness hung on. Even after five months, he was still too weak to return to the vigorous life of a sailor. His mother prayed that her son would see the error of his ways and repent. She asked James to pray also, but he was not quite ready to do so. To help him pass the time, Eliza borrowed every available book for James. After he had read them all at least twice, she then brought in Sam Bates, a young teacher, to teach James arithmetic and spelling. She kept hoping that her beloved son would give up the wayward life of a sailor and go back to school.

GEAUGA SEMINARY

In those days, children were taught basic reading, writing, and arithmetic in a district school. To continue their education, they had to attend a private institution before they could enter college. Young Sam Bates was a student at Geauga Seminary, a religious school conducted by the Free Will Baptists. He convinced Orrin Judd and William Boynton, James' cousin, to go to Geauga for the spring term. Eliza offered James 17 dollars — the entire household savings — if he would join them. James agreed, vowing that when he was strong enough to return to work on the canal, he would repay every penny.

On March 6, 1849, wearing a faded wool shirt, patched pants, and a ragged straw hat, James set out for Geauga Seminary with William and Orrin. Carrying their supplies of food as well as quilts and extra clothing, the boys walked 10 miles to Chester, Ohio.

Geauga Seminary was only a wooden building on a bluff overlooking the Chagrin River, but to James it seemed impressive. He was delighted with the variety of courses the school offered. Because there was a fee ranging from 50 cents to two dollars for each course, he carefully selected algebra, philosophy, and grammar. The glee club was free, however, and later he debated in several Greek societies.

James shared a rented room with Orrin and William. It cost each boy about a dollar a week. Because they had to buy a stove and pay for books and other supplies, James did odd jobs in order to make his 17 dollars stretch to the end of the term.

Boarding school was the best medicine for James. He had never felt happier, stronger, or more independent. When the term was over, he spent the summer haying and carpentering, counting the days until the next school term would begin. James was not so sure he wanted to go back to the canal now. He had become fascinated with learning.

Chapter 2

Teaching and Preaching

In 1850, two months before his 18th birthday, James was hired to teach at the district school in Solon, Ohio. Some of his pupils were not much younger than he was. One day he asked a 16-year-old boy to read in front of the class. The fellow refused. Again James commanded him to stand up and read. When the boy did not move, the younger children began to snicker. It made their teacher angry. Although he hated to resort to flogging, James grabbed his whip, stomped over, and pulled the disobedient boy to his feet. In his journal James wrote of the incident, "I flogged him severely and told him to take his seat. He caught a billet [stick] of wood and came at me, and we had a merry time." At the end of the term, however, James had earned the respect of his students for being a good teacher and for maintaining discipline.

BECOMING A TEACHER

Before James became a teacher in Solon, he went back to Geauga Seminary in August of 1849 for the fall term and worked part-time for a carpenter. When the term ended late in October, James looked for work to make some money before school began again in March. But there was no work to be found. The harvest was already in, there were no jobs on the canal, and nobody needed a carpenter.

Geauga Seminary closed for a winter recess because that was the time when farm children went to school. The Geauga students could then get jobs teaching at the district schools. James had not planned on teaching, but because there was nothing else for him to do, he took an examination and earned his teacher's certificate.

Looking for a teaching job proved very disagreeable for James. Every time he was turned down, he felt hurt and embarrassed. Eventually, however, he found a position in Solon, near his home. James taught all grades and children of all ages. But because he was young and inexperienced, he had many discipline problems. Yet, by learning to control his students, James was also learning to control his own temper.

Leaving Geauga

When the spring term began, James returned to Geauga and studied Latin, botany, and algebra. Then in October 1850, he left the seminary and taught school in Warrensville, Ohio, and worked as a carpenter for the next year. James left Geauga because of a religious disagreement between the Disciples and the Baptists. He had gone through a conversion and a baptism (a ceremony by which he was cleansed of sin and committed to the Disciples). Because of this deep religious experience, he had denounced the evil life on the canal, where he had been "ripe for ruin." To lead a purer life, James gave up cursing and never swore again, even later when he was in the army. He was serious about his religion.

THE ECLECTIC INSTITUTE

In the fall of 1851, accompanied by Orrin Judd and four of his cousins, James entered the Western Reserve Eclectic Institute (later called Hiram College) at Hiram, Ohio. Eclectic meant that the institute offered a variety of philosophical and intellectual studies. The square, red brick school had an impressive name, but up until the preceding year the campus had been nothing more than a cornfield. There was virtually no housing, and the school was purposely located far from roads leading to "urban temptations." James had chosen the Eclectic because it was run by the Disciples. To earn money, he took a job as the institute janitor for two terms. Then, in the spring of 1852, James was asked to teach in the Eclectic's elementary school.

Because of the haphazard way young Garfield had selected his subjects at Geauga, he had to work hard to complete the required junior college studies. When he was not teaching, he spent hours studying. He became a classical scholar and read many books in Latin and Greek. Although he studied ancient politics and war, he showed no interest in current politics. When Franklin Pierce ran against Winfield Scott for President in 1852, James Garfield wrote he was glad he was not old enough to vote because he hated politics and politicians.

Friendships and Romance

At this time James was almost six feet tall, a strong, broad-shouldered young man. He could outwrestle and outrun most of his classmates. James was also becoming a fine orator whose words had great power to move people. Because he was outgoing and had a heart as one friend said, "as big as a milk pail," he was very popular.

One of James' best friends at the Eclectic was Almeda A. Booth. She was a plain woman, eight years older than James, whose sharp mind stimulated him to learn. The two scholars were far ahead of the others in their class. James often said that next to his mother Almeda had the most influence on his thinking, reasoning, and living.

Almeda may have stimulated his mind, but James became romantically involved with Mary Hubbell, a girl who was lively, warm, and full of fun. She was a former pupil of James' at the Warrensville district school and the daughter of a prominent Disciple. They were together so much that everyone expected them to get married. But James was not ready for marriage. In fact, the prospect of marriage in his early twenties frightened him. So, after much soul-searching, James broke off with Mary. The Hubbell family was outraged, believing he had jilted their daughter. It created an unpleasant situation that made James very unhappy. He threw himself into his work, studying 18 hours a day.

Preaching for the Disciples

In the church of the Disciples, members were sometimes invited to give sermons. Because of James' deep faith and his reputation for being a powerful orator, in the spring of 1853 he was asked to give a sermon in a nearby church. Toward the end of the year, he was preaching almost every Sunday in a different church. He received a gold dollar for each sermon.

IMPORTANT DECISIONS

The scars of his painful romance with Mary Hubbell were barely beginning to fade when James became interested in another young lady, Lucretia Rudolph (nicknamed Crete). Lucretia, a dark-eyed beauty of quiet charm and delicate health, was the daughter of Zeb Rudolph, a leading Hiram

Disciple. Although Crete had been James' classmate at Geauga, she was now a pupil in a Greek class that he was teaching at the Eclectic Institute. In November 1853, he began writing her letters, and by the following spring they were in love.

It was a strange romance. Although James professed to love Lucretia, he did not want to marry her. He was not sure she had the warmth he needed in a wife. Besides, he wanted to go on with his schooling before he settled down.

When James finished the Eclectic Institute, he did not have enough money to continue his education. So he took a full-time teaching position and saved most of his salary for college. James was considering going to Bethany College in Virginia because it was headed by the Disciples' founder and leader, Alexander Campbell. But although Campbell had impressed him when he had visited there in the summer of 1853, the college had been a disappointment. He disliked the students' southern manners, and he was shocked when he saw would-be preachers putting on theatricals.

For an entire year, James mulled over the pros and cons of attending Bethany College. He could earn a degree there in 10 months, whereas it would take at least two years if he attended a New England college. Going to Bethany would probably mean a Disciple-centered life leading to a preaching career. Would he then become a person who looked at things from one narrow point of view? James did not want to be that kind of person. He was eager to learn more about the world, he said, "for the sake of liberalizing my mind." A broader education would be best, he decided, so he applied to Yale, Brown, and Williams College. Each school would have accepted him with the same requirements for graduation. But because the reply from President Mark Hopkins of Williams had concluded with the sentence, "If you come here we shall do what we can for you," James settled on Williams College.

WILLIAMS COLLEGE

In July 1854, James went to Williamstown, a little town in the Berkshire hills of western Massachusetts where Williams College was located, to take an informal entrance exam. After translating Latin and Greek texts and solving a few geometry problems, he was admitted to the junior class at Williams. James was eager to start college life, but classes did not begin for two months.

In the fall, James joined the student body of 231 young men. He feasted his mind on subjects such as geology, astronomy, and history, and mastered both the written and spoken German language in his first year. He was not only an avid reader of Shakespeare's works, but he kept abreast of all the current publications of poetry and fiction.

Friendships at Williams

James' roommate and close friend, Charles Wilber, was a handicapped fellow who was also from Ohio. The two from the West attracted attention because their dress and talk were different from the others. Their classmates also noted that James and Charles were members of the Disciples, which they thought was an odd and quite radical religion.

Once James demonstrated his skill in debate, however, he made many friends. Before organized sports, the debating team was the focus of collegiate activity. A good debater always brought fame to his school. "Garfield was undoubtedly one of the greatest debaters ever seen at Williams College," one of his classmates said. He saw James as a person whose "magnificent bursts of fiery eloquence won and held the attention of his audience from the moment he opened his lips." James debated all the important issues of the day, such as the fate of Kansas, the dangers of immigration, and the Crimean War (between Russia and the armies of France, England, Sardinia, and Turkey).

A change was coming over James at Williams. As he took part in the horseplay and practical jokes of his new college friends, he was losing his prudish attitude. His new friends were becoming more tolerant of him, too. They even admitted that a Disciple could be a sincere Christian.

In each of his activities, James was chosen to be the leader. Despite opposition of the fraternities, he was elected president of the Philogian Society, a major campus literary society. He was also elected editor of the *Williams Quarterly,* a high-quality literary magazine. Before long, James became a campus politician who never lost an election at Williams College.

Summer Vacation

In 1855, at the end of his junior year, James returned to Ohio boasting newly grown, chestnut-colored whiskers. During his vacation he went to see Crete. But when they were together, James again felt that she was lacking in warmth. Crete, who had always concealed her feelings, did not know how to show James her love. Finally she gave him her private diary. What she could not tell him face-to-face, she had written in her journal.

When James read Crete's diary, he saw how deeply she cared for him. By the time he left to return to Williams, they were engaged to be married. However, James was a romanticist who liked women, and there were other women with whom he would become involved before he settled down with Crete.

Becoming Involved

James' academic record at Williams was not outstanding, but he was in the upper half of his class. One of the courses he enjoyed most was taught by President Mark Hopkins. Instead of just listening to the president lecture, the students were encouraged to think for themselves—even argue with him. James, who loved a good debate, thought Hopkins was an outstanding teacher.

In November of his senior year, James attended a lecture on political issues. Listening to Congressman John Z. Goodrich, a Republican from Massachusetts, talk about the Kansas-Nebraska struggle (a fight between the North and South as to whether a new state joining the Union would be slave or free), James realized he knew nothing of this important issue. But he vowed to find out about it. He told a friend, "At such hours as this I feel like throwing the whole current of my life into the work of opposing this giant evil."

James studied the Missouri Compromise of 1820 (a law making the southern boundary of Missouri the future dividing line between slave and free states in the Louisiana Purchase territory) and all the constitutional questions involved in slavery. When he had considered the issues, he leaned toward the Republican Party and their policies. Contrary to the teachings of his religion, he was becoming involved in politics. This was quite a turnabout for James, who had once said that he hated politics.

AT A CROSSROAD

Officially, James was still going to be a Disciple preacher. But as graduation drew near, he found himself at the intersection of life and faith. He began to question his intended career on theological and monetary grounds. In the spring of 1856, he admitted to Crete that although he still remained a devoted Disciple, "the distracted and disorganized state of the Brotherhood rather repels me from them and renders the ministry an uncompromising field." By the middle of June he had made up his mind. "I think I shall not become a preacher now, if I ever do," he said. Yet James did not turn to politics right away. He was looking forward to his graduation, and afterward he planned to teach at the Eclectic Institute in Hiram.

On August 7, 1856, James A. Garfield was graduated from Williams College. His fiancee, Lucretia Rudolph, was at the exercises. So were other friends, including Rebecca Selleck, a pretty young woman with whom James recently had had a love affair. James was graduated with honors and gave an eloquent commencement oration. He had reached his goal. He had earned a degree from one of the best colleges in America, and now he was going to be an educator.

Chapter 3
Political Beginnings

J ames Garfield was 25 years old in 1856 when he rejoined the faculty of the Eclectic Institute in Hiram. He soon saw that the staff was overworked and edgy. And because of President Hayden's frequent absences and loose supervision, the little Disciple school was in trouble academically and financially. "Had I known before all I now know," Garfield said, "I would not have come here at all." After his success at Williams, he felt a tremendous letdown at the Eclectic. He was moody and unhappy and vowed if things did not improve he would leave when his one-year contract expired.

Garfield taught Latin, Greek, and English grammar. He was an inspiring teacher, well-liked by his students. His teaching load was heavy—six classes a day and sometimes more, but he was not afraid of work. As he once told a class, "Gentlemen, I can express my creed of life in one word, 'I believe in work, I BELIEVE IN WORK.' " Garfield's method of teaching was advanced for his day. He followed President Hopkins' example and encouraged his students to think for themselves.

COLLEGE PRESIDENT

In May 1857, President Hayden was forced to retire. Normally his position would have been given to Professor Norman Dunshee, the senior member of the Eclectic faculty. But when Garfield's name was also brought up for consideration, the trustees of the institute could not agree on the man to take Hayden's place. To solve the problem, they created a board of education made up of the five teachers who comprised the faculty. When the board met, they elected Garfield chairman. The title of president soon followed.

This promotion hardly took Garfield by surprise. His interest in being the institute's president was so obvious earlier that Crete had cautioned him not to rush things. But Garfield claimed that he had accepted the position only at the urging of the trustees.

As president, James kept up an almost impossible pace. Although he received no increase in salary, he was expected to continue teaching his classes and perform all presidential duties. Being an ordained minister, he was also in demand at Disciple churches, where people flocked to hear his eloquent orations. He lectured on scientific and literary subjects too, and spoke at teacher institutes. It was no wonder that he complained, "My head throbs wearily and my tired heart and body are calling for rest. . . . "

Growing Restless

Under Garfield's leadership, the Eclectic prospered. Enrollment rose, and the school was at last financially sound. However, as James' presidency stretched into two and then three years, he became increasingly restless. He searched for another career that would interest him more. But he did not know what else to do with his life. He told Crete, "The decision must come before long." Then he pleaded, "In the meantime all who love me can aid me by support and forebearance."

Crete had been more than patient. She had waited for over four years of an embarrassingly long engagement for James to marry her. But Garfield kept delaying the wedding because he felt that "the narrow exclusiveness of marriage" would limit his circle of friends. He wanted to keep up his friendships with Rebecca Selleck, Almeda Booth, and others. Charles Wilber told him he was neglecting Crete. James denied it, saying, "If I ever marry, I expect to marry Lucretia Rudolph." Nevertheless, he did not break off with the other women.

MARRIAGE AT LAST

James finally realized that sooner or later he would have to marry Crete. If he did not, the rumors of loose morals that had hung over him ever since his relationship with Mary Hubbell would surface again. So, on November 11, 1858, James A. Garfield and Lucretia Rudolph were married in a quiet ceremony at the bride's home. Strangely, James asked a Presbyterian minister rather than a Disciple preacher to marry them. Immediately after the wedding, the newlyweds moved into Mrs. Northrup's boardinghouse across from the Hiram campus. Almeda Booth's room was right next door. Almost everywhere the new Mr. and Mrs. Garfield went, Almeda went too. Crete tried her best to make James happy, but it did not happen during the three years they lived at Mrs. Northrup's.

Debating Evolution

A few weeks after his marriage, Garfield gained fame by debating evolution (the origin and development of the world) with an Englishman named William Denton. Denton was a well-known lecturer who debated widely on the subject. He believed that man, animals, and vegetables came from "spontaneous generation and progressive development without the help of God."

Garfield read all of his opponent's works and took cram courses in geology, botany, zoology, astronomy, and anthropology. He sent friends to hear the fiery Denton speak and take notes. Finally, he was ready to confront the man who intended "to invalidate the claims of the Bible and remove God from immediate control of the universe." The debating sessions began on December 27 in Chagrin, Ohio, and lasted until New Year's Eve. People flocked to hear the preacher challenge the scientist. When it was over, James Garfield's reputation as a defender of the faith was firmly established. Yet, as a result of his scientific studies, Garfield reluctantly had to admit that the world was millions of years old.

The Dunshee Matter

At the Eclectic, there was an undercurrent of criticism of Garfield's policies as well as his character. Garfield suspected that Norman Dunshee, his former rival for the school's presidency, was behind it. Dunshee also demanded that the Eclectic adopt a stronger stand against slavery. When Garfield refused to do so, Dunshee openly opposed him. Garfield told the trustees about his differences with the professor, and Dunshee was fired. Angrily, Dunshee accused Garfield of planning his dismissal because of his antislavery views.

Garfield replied that he did not "directly counsel" the professor's dismissal nor had he expected it. A month earlier, however, he had written J. Harrison (Harry) Rhodes, a former teacher at the Eclectic then studying at Williams College, urging him to return to Hiram. "If you do this," Garfield wrote, "I think the trustees would dispense with Norman soon and your salary would be a fair one." Professor Dunshee left Hiram under protest and Harry Rhodes became the professor's replacement.

FIRST STIRRINGS OF POLITICS

Although Garfield was now secure as president at the Eclectic, he was dissatisfied with academic life and all of its bickering. He thought about becoming a lawyer. But if the Disciple ministers knew he was studying law, he could lose everything he had worked for. So Garfield continued to teach and preach, and he studied law privately. As time went on, he also became interested in politics. Yet he would not seek political office – that was not his way.

In early August 1859, Garfield received an honorary master's degree from Williams College. Soon after, a committee of Ohio Republicans asked him to run for state senator to represent the counties of Summit and Portage. Garfield had been known as a Republican ever since 1856, when he had favored Republican John Fremont for President. He agreed to let the committee place his name in nomination.

Winning the Nomination

Summit County was a Republican stronghold. But Portage, where Garfield lived and the Eclectic was located, was divided between the radical new Republican Party and the conservative Democrats. At the party caucuses (closed meetings of members of a political party to make policy decisions and select candidates for office), the delegates wanted to nominate a man who had not spoken out on the slavery issue. Garfield had not. And the dismissal of Professor Dunshee further emphasized Garfield's conservatism on the abolition (antislavery) issue. So, on August 16, 1859, James A. Garfield was chosen over three other men to run for state senator.

The Republican state convention met on August 26 and accepted the caucus choice. They made it seem that although Garfield had not sought the office, they had nominated him because he stood out far above the rest.

However, many powerful leaders of the Disciples were against Garfield mixing into politics. Politics, they said, was too lowly an occupation for a man of faith. Garfield pointed out that he had not sought the office, he had been drafted. Then, assuring the church leaders that a man could be both a gentleman and a politician, he said, "I believe that I can enter political life and retain my integrity, manhood, and religion. I believe that there is vastly more need of manly men in politics than of preachers." Garfield further soothed their fears by telling them he thought of himself as a school principal taking a leave of absence for two terms. His convincing words won him the support of the religious community.

The Campaign for State Senator

In Garfield's district, slavery was the most important issue in the campaign. An incident had occurred at Oberlin, Ohio, where an abolitionist mob tried to stop authorities from enforcing the Fugitive Slave Act (a strict federal law for the arrest of runaway slaves—offering rewards for the capture of people who helped them). The mob had snatched a fugitive slave away from the federal marshals. Some of the rescuers were also involved in the Underground Railroad, a secret network of people who helped slaves escape to Canada. The abolitionists were found guilty and sentenced to prison for violating the Fugitive Slave Law. The case went all the way to the Ohio Supreme Court, but the verdict was upheld.

Republicans were especially angry with Judge Swan, the only Republican member of the Ohio Supreme Court, who had agreed with the Democrats. Candidate James Garfield was now forced to speak out on the issue. Although he personally did not like the Fugitive Slave Law, Garfield said that because the judges were bound by the law and the precedents set by the federal courts, they had made the correct decision. His stand antagonized the radical Republicans. For the rest

Harriet Tubman—Moses of Her People

Harriet Ross Tubman was a black woman who did much to help her people. She was born into slavery sometime in 1821 on a plantation in Dorchester County, Maryland. She had no schooling and worked as a field hand doing hard labor.

In 1844 her master forced Harriet to marry another slave, John Tubman. Day in and day out she saw the evils of slavery around her. Two of her sisters had been sold, and she had been beaten. Harriet longed for freedom. When she was about 27 years old, she ran away to Philadelphia and found a job as a cook. Then she heard about the Underground Railroad. It was not really underground, nor was it a railroad. It was a secret system whereby antislavery people helped escaped slaves reach Canada. They provided hiding places or "stations" along the routes used by the fugitive slaves.

Despite the Fugitive Slave Act and the $40,000 reward offered for her capture, Harriet Tubman made 19 trips over the Underground Railroad into slave territory. Widely respected for her courage and strength in leading more than 300 slaves to freedom, Harriet earned the name "Moses of Her People." In 1857 she freed her elderly parents and brought them to New York. Although she had never learned to read or write, Harriet was a popular speaker at antislavery meetings.

When the Civil War broke out, Harriet served the Union army as a cook and nurse. Few people knew she was also a scout and spy, going back and forth over familiar territory behind Confederate lines.

After the war, Harriet Tubman lived in Auburn, New York, and worked to improve the lives of former slaves. She turned her home into a home for aged and needy blacks. After she died on March 10, 1913, the people of Auburn erected a monument in memory of their Moses.

of the campaign, they attacked Garfield as bitterly as the Democrats did, calling him a "conservative." Yet, despite their opposition, on election day, October 11, 1859, Garfield won by 1,430 votes.

STATE SENATOR GARFIELD

James A. Garfield, the freshman senator from Ohio's 26th District arrived in Columbus, the state capital, on the last day of 1859. He was met by William Bascom, a prominent Republican at whose home he was to board. Jacob Dolson Cox, the new senator from the district adjacent to Garfield's was also staying at Bascom's. The two young senators took a liking to one another and soon became good friends.

At 28, Garfield was the youngest member of the Ohio legislature. He was not planning to make a speech at the first session, but a bill to cut funds for school libraries came up. Loving books as he did, Garfield could not help speaking

out against the measure. Although the bill passed, his eloquence won him the attention he craved. Once Garfield had
a taste of speaking before the legislature, he had something
to say about almost every bill.

Taking a Stand

The voters back home were well aware of Garfield's eloquence, but they were becoming impatient. They wanted him
to take a stand against slavery. So when a bill was introduced
to prohibit military expeditions from Ohio into other states,
Garfield blasted the measure. The bill was a result of a raid
by a fanatic abolitionist named John Brown on Harper's Ferry,
Virginia. (Brown had been convicted of treason and hanged
for leading a war party that captured the town and the U.S.
armory there.) In the South, Brown was considered to be a
criminal. In the North, and especially in Garfield's district,
Brown was a hero.

Despite Garfield's "radical" views, Governor William
Dennison chose him to invite Kentucky and Tennessee to a
peace meeting with Ohio. The combined Kentucky and Tennessee legislatures heard Garfield's forceful plea for unity of
the three western states on the Mississippi River. He was careful not to alienate the slaveowners of these border states or
to destroy abolitionist support in his own district. The mission was a great social success but not much else was
accomplished.

Back in Hiram

After the legislative session ended in the spring of 1860,
Garfield went home to Hiram. Harry Rhodes had kept things
running at the Eclectic, but Garfield was still president, and
there were many matters that needed his attention. There were
also problems to face at home.

Garfield had not taken his wife with him to Columbus. He had told her he would be too busy with legislative duties to spend time with her. Crete felt neglected, and when she tried to talk about it with her husband, he hurt her more by saying that he thought their marriage was "a great mistake." Crete begged him not to blame her for her feelings. ". . . I crush back tears, as long as I can," she told him, "for I know they make you unhappy."

James was very unhappy. Deep inside he felt a "sadness almost bordering on despair," he said. But that summer he and Crete tried hard to patch up their differences, for they were expecting a child. On July 3, 1860, Crete gave birth to a daughter, Eliza, whom the delighted parents nicknamed Trot.

LINCOLN ELECTED

The day after Trot was born, her father was off to Ravenna, Ohio, fulfilling a commitment to deliver an address. In his speech, Garfield scoffed at the open threats of secession southerners had made should Abraham Lincoln of Illinois be elected President. Lincoln had been nominated at the Republican National Convention in May. Garfield's Ravenna address was the first of over 50 political speeches he made for the Republican ticket during the presidential campaign of 1860.

The Democratic Party had broken apart over the slavery question. Northern Democrats had nominated Stephen A. Douglas of Illinois for President, and a group of southern Democrats had selected John C. Breckenridge of Kentucky. Wherever he talked, in tents, churches, outdoor groves, or town halls, Garfield railed against slavery. He also denounced the "squatter's sovereignty" doctrine (the right of the people who moved into new territories to decide whether to allow slavery to exist there) of candidate Douglas. William Bascom followed his boarder's career with interest. As chairman of the Ohio Central Republican Committee and secretary to Governor Dennison, he was delighted with Garfield's success.

Cheering crowds who thronged to hear Senator Garfield saw him as a good-looking, robust six-footer with light hair and whiskers. His unusually large head gave him a powerful look. But his forceful voice and eloquent speaking style were his greatest assets. The more Garfield spoke, the more his self-esteem grew. He gradually became his good-natured, unpredictable self again. The Garfields found much joy in their baby daughter, and they drew closer together because of her.

On election day, November 6, 1860, the Republicans carried Ohio, and Garfield noted in his diary, "Voted for Lincoln and Hamlin. Went to Ravenna in evening; at midnight knew that L. and H. were elected. God be praised!" Abraham Lincoln had won a majority of the electoral college votes (people chosen from each state to elect the U.S. President and Vice-President) but not a majority of the popular vote.

The South Secedes

The issues dividing the country had come down to sectional rivalry and slavery. On December 20, 1860, a little over a month after Lincoln's election, South Carolina, long the leading voice of rebellion, voted to secede from the Union. Mississippi followed on January 9, and then Florida, Alabama, Georgia, and Louisiana. Garfield finally saw that nothing "this side of a miracle of God" could prevent a civil war.

The seceded states met in February 1861 to form a provisional government, and Texas left the Union. Jefferson Davis was made the president of the Confederate States of America. The inaction of the Buchanan administration filled

Garfield, the former pacifist, with anger. He wanted the federal government to arm and defend the Union. But Congress was desperately searching for a compromise. The country was in an upheaval, but in spite of it Garfield continued to read law. Early in 1861, he was admitted to the Ohio bar (able to practice law in that state).

The Civil War Begins

In February, President-elect Abraham Lincoln stopped in Columbus, Ohio, on his way to Washington for his inauguration. The citizens wanted strong talk from him against the states that had defied the federal government. Instead, Lincoln gave a mild, disappointing speech. Garfield cautioned people to give Lincoln time. He found him to be ". . . frank, direct and thoroughly honest," Garfield said. "His remarkable good sense, simple and condensed style of expression, and evident marks of indomitable will, give me great hopes for the country." Yet later, after a weak inaugural address, even Senator Garfield grew impatient with his leader. Unsure of the loyalty of the federal troops, Lincoln had to be cautious. Besides, there was little money in the federal treasury to finance a war.

As Lincoln marked time, Garfield was busy campaigning for Governor Dennison for U.S. senator. When Dennison was defeated, Garfield was so unhappy he considered giving up politics. Then, on April 12, 1861, while Garfield was attending a session of the state senate, a senator burst in waving a telegram. "Mr. President," the senator shouted, "the telegraph announces that the secessionists are bombarding Fort Sumter!" There was a deathly silence in the room. Fort Sumter was a large fort about six miles southeast of Charleston, South Carolina, then occupied by federal troops. The inevitable Civil War had finally begun.

Chapter 4
Off to War

D ue to pressure from the press and from Congress, Union soldiers were ordered to attack Richmond, Virginia, on July 21, 1861. General Winfield Scott, the Union commander, knew his raw recruits were not ready for combat. Yet the militiamen and their elected officers, hoping to bring a quick end to the war, insisted on going ahead with the plan. Washington officials expected to see the southern forces demolished by the Union troops, and they drove their coaches up to the combat line to watch the fun. Much to their surprise, the Confederates took a stand near a small stream called Bull Run, just south of Washington, D.C. After a hard fight, they defeated the untrained Union soldiers. Northerners were not so sure now that the war would be over by harvest time.

EARLY MONTHS OF THE WAR

Fort Sumter surrendered to the Confederates on April 13, 1861. James Garfield hoped Lincoln would now declare war because he thought it was the only way to destroy slavery and preserve the Union. The President declared a state of insurrection instead, to prevent foreign powers from recognizing the Confederacy as a nation. Two days after Lincoln's declaration, Virginia left the Union. Arkansas seceded on May

6, and it seemed that North Carolina and Tennessee were soon likely to follow. Not a shot had been fired since Fort Sumter, but there was no doubt that the war had begun.

At first it was feared that the Confederates would march on the nation's capital. But a call for 75,000 volunteers to serve a three-month stint in the Union Army brought thousands of recruits into Washington. As a result, northerners became confident that they would win the war very soon. But the feeling in the South was just as confident. Southerners thought of the war as a challenge to their strong sense of honor. Hundreds of experienced southern fighting men resigned from their positions in the Union Army and returned to their home states in the South to offer their services to the Confederacy.

Lieutenant Colonel Garfield

During the early months of the war, the burden of defending the Union fell almost entirely on the individual states. State Senators Garfield and Jacob Dolson Cox helped Governor Dennison map out plans for Ohio's part in the war. The state legislature rushed through emergency measures, including a large state loan to raise and equip the militiamen who were pouring into Columbus.

Garfield, filled with patriotism, read dozens of military books until he thought he knew enough about war to be commissioned a high-ranking officer. In late April of 1861, he helped recruit men for the Seventh Regiment of the Ohio Volunteer Infantry and hoped to become their colonel. At that time, three-month men elected their officers, so Garfield ran for the post against Colonel Erastus B. Tyler, a 23-year militiaman. Tyler was elected while Garfield was away on a mission for the governor. When Garfield returned, he charged that Tyler had used "bargain and brandy" to get votes. He wanted to contest the election, but friends persuaded him that it would hurt his political prospects. Garfield then tried for another command, but again he was unsuccessful.

As the war went on, President Lincoln realized that the Union needed an army of trained men who would enlist for longer than three months. He began raising forces of volunteers who agreed to serve for three years. As these units were activated, they replaced the three-month militia. The officers of the three-year units were political appointees chosen for their ability to raise money and men. In mid-June, Governor Dennison offered Garfield an appointment as lieutenant colonel in an Ohio regiment. Garfield was disappointed. His friend, Jacob Cox, had been made a brigadier general, a much higher rank than lieutenant colonel, so he declined. Garfield's recent defeats had made him feel depressed again, and he needed time to pull himself together.

In July Garfield went on a trip to visit family and friends in other states. While he was away, he kept up with the war news. It was shocking to hear about the rout of the Union troops at Bull Run. When Garfield returned to Ohio, he found a letter from Governor Dennison offering him the lieutenant colonelcy of a new Ohio regiment. The rank was no higher than the first one he had been offered, but this time he accepted. On August 16, 1861, State Senator James A. Garfield was sworn in as lieutenant colonel of the 42nd Ohio Volunteer Infantry. He was assigned to Camp Chase near Columbus. After three weeks of camp duty, study, and practicing horsemanship, Governor Dennison appointed 30-year-old Garfield a full colonel in command of the 42nd Ohio.

COLONEL JAMES GARFIELD

The 42nd Ohio Volunteer Infantry did not really exist, except on paper. It was Garfield's duty to recruit men and organize his regiment. He appointed Lionel A. Sheldon as

General James A. Garfield proudly poses with his staff of officers during the Civil War. (Library of Congress.)

lieutenant colonel and Don Albert Pardee as major of the regiment to help him. For recruits, Garfield turned to the students and graduates of the Eclectic. Many of them had been awaiting their school president's commission so they could fight under his command. Garfield was impressive in his blue uniform as he stood before them at the village church urging them to sign up. They did not need any persuasion, and the Hiram, Ohio, boys were soon mustered in as Company A. They were the first of Garfield's troops to arrive at Camp Chase.

By October, Colonel Garfield's regiment consisted of six companies, but he needed still more men. It was not until late November that the regiment reached its full strength of 1,000 men—10 companies.

On Active Duty

On December 14, the 42nd Ohio Volunteer Infantry Regiment was called to active duty. Although Garfield had been impatient to see action, he bid a tender good-bye to Crete and Trot and worried that his little daughter would not remember him if he did not return.

The 42nd went by train to Cincinnati. There, Garfield worked half the night loading gear, horses, wagons, supplies, and 150 wild mules onto two small steamers. His regiment was to board the crowded steamers and head up the river to Catlettsburg, Kentucky, at the mouth of the Big Sandy River. Colonel Garfield did not plan to accompany his men, for he had received orders to report to army headquarters at Louisville, Kentucky.

Leaving Sheldon in command of his troops, Garfield reported to Brigadier General Don Carlos Buell, commander of the Department of the Ohio. General Buell's army stretched across the southern half of Kentucky from the Mississippi River to the Cumberland Mountains. Although his military objective was to take Nashville, Tennessee, he had not planned any action until spring. Circumstances, however, forced him to change his mind.

Stopping General Marshall

General Humphrey Marshall and a large Confederate force had sneaked through a gap in the Cumberland Mountains and were making their way down the Sandy Valley on the Kentucky side. Marshall's brigade was a threat to General Buell's left flank. Buell needed a strong commander to drive Marshall back before the Union troops could move on to Nashville.

One of Buell's officers, Colonel William B. Hazen, had been a student at the Eclectic before he went to the United States Military Academy at West Point, New York. Hazen suggested James Garfield for the job, and Buell approved. It was an odd choice because the general did not know Garfield. Besides, Garfield had been a soldier for less than six months. Yet his inexperience did not seem to bother General Buell. When Colonel Garfield stood before the general neatly uniformed and wearing a magnificent sword, Buell was favorably impressed. He outlined the problem and asked Garfield to come up with a detailed plan of attack to stop General Marshall.

Garfield was overwhelmed with the task before him. He had never seen a battle, never even heard an enemy gun, and here he was, a country schoolmaster, responsible for an important military campaign! He went to his hotel room armed with the maps and papers Buell had given him and worked all through the night.

A Plan for Battle

Because his command encompassed 6,000 square miles of wilderness without railroads or telegraph lines, Garfield figured that supplies would be the key to winning or losing the battle. Having been a canal boy, he knew that if he stayed close to the river he could bring in supplies by water. Because General Marshall would have to haul his supplies over the treacherous mountains from Virginia, his advance would be slow.

Garfield worked out a plan which General Buell approved. Garfield's regiment, the 42nd Ohio, was to join with what remained of Colonel Moore's 14th Kentucky. They were to go up the valley until they met the Confederates and block their advance. Meanwhile, the 40th Ohio, under the command of Colonel Jonathan Cranor, was to march east from Paris, Kentucky, where they were camped, to the upper Sandy Valley, sneak behind the Confederate lines, and at exactly the same moment, the two armies would crush the enemy troops in a pincer movement.

Garfield was also assigned four cavalry squadrons, mostly from Kentucky, and the 16th Ohio Infantry, which was kept in reserve at Lexington, Kentucky. Theoretically, Garfield could have had more than 3,000 men under his command, but he would fight with about half that number.

It was rumored that General Marshall had already reached Prestonburg, Kentucky, and that Colonel Moore's 14th Kentucky had retreated to Catlettsburg, at the mouth of the Big Sandy River. Garfield sprang into action. He rode to Colonel Cranor's camp, gave the 40th their orders, and then boarded a steamer in Cincinnati, Ohio, to join his regiment. When he arrived in Catlettsburg on December 20, he found that his regiment and the two Kentucky regiments had moved on to Louisa, Kentucky, a tiny village about 30 miles upstream. Garfield rejoined his troops there.

THE BATTLE OF THE BIG SANDY

While Garfield's forces rested at Louisa, scouts brought back reports that Marshall had between 2,000 and 2,500 men in an elevated position beyond the village of Paintsville, Kentucky, and there were also about 300 to 400 Confederate cavalry at another camp on Jenny's Creek. The only reliable soldiers Garfield had were the 1,000 raw recruits in his 42nd

Ohio, but at least they had guns. His 500 Kentuckians in Colonel Moore's regiment were not only untrained but were poorly armed as well. And his Kentucky cavalry, also untrained and unarmed, could not be depended on for more than scouting duty.

With the 40th Ohio under Colonel Cranor still hundreds of miles away, Garfield could see how dangerous his plan was. He was in an isolated mountain region, the weather was bitter, and the roads were ribbons of mud. Garfield sent Colonel Cranor orders to cut south toward Prestonburg, Kentucky, but he had no way of knowing if the colonel had received his orders. Relying on messengers riding through a state where the people were as likely to be sympathetic to Confederate as to Union soldiers was taking a big chance.

The Attack on Paintsville

Days went by, and Garfield did not hear from his messenger or Colonel Cranor. He knew the risks involved in attacking Marshall, but Garfield was eager for action. On December 23, against the advice of his staff, he mounted his horse, Billy, and commanded his troops to move out. Garfield led his men over the rough terrain, through mud and rain, gaining only 10 miles that day. Yet they kept on going, and on New Year's Day, 1862, Garfield's messenger caught up with them. He reported that the 40th Ohio was advancing, but it was still quite far away. Nevertheless, Garfield was pleased to have made contact.

On January 4, 1862, Garfield's Union troops reached the outskirts of Paintsville, where he was happy to find temporary cavalry reinforcements waiting. They had been sent by his friend, Jacob Cox. Cox, stationed in a nearby valley, was now a major general in charge of operations. His highly trained cavalrymen, commanded by Colonel William M.

Bolles, were on loan for only a few days. Garfield knew that if he was going to attack Marshall he had to move quickly.

The next day, Garfield divided his force into three small detachments. He then placed cavalry in front of each group to make the force seem larger than it was and sent them down each of the three roads leading to Paintsville. Garfield planned to chase the Confederates from the town and link forces with Cranor there. General Marshall, thinking a large force was moving against him on all three roads, ordered his army to leave Paintsville. His men made a hasty exit to a fortified position three miles south. While Marshall's army waited behind the fortifications, scouts brought them word that Cranor's 40th Ohio was closing in on them. Once more Marshall retreated up the valley.

The Battle of Jenny's Creek

In the meantime, Colonel Garfield's troops entered Paintsville. Finding the village deserted, Garfield sent Colonel Bolles and his cavalry up Jenny's Creek to fight the rebel cavalry that was camped there. With the rest of his men, Garfield occupied Marshall's empty fort. Then an urgent message came through from Colonel Bolles that he had sighted the enemy cavalry and was ready to attack. Garfield sent word for Bolles to hold off until he could bring help.

Assembling a force of 400 men, Garfield struck out for Jenny's Creek. The plan was his old favorite. While Colonel Bolles fought the enemy, Garfield would attack their rear. But Colonel Bolles did not wait for Garfield. Instead, he attacked the rebel cavalry, killed six men, wounded several more, and once again the Confederates scattered. When Garfield's men arrived, tired and cold, the battle was already over. They had trudged 13 miles, waded across icy streams, climbed hill after hill, and struggled through frozen mud. Now they had to turn around and go back to camp.

THE BATTLE OF MIDDLE CREEK

Upon returning to camp, Garfield found Colonel Cranor and the 40th Ohio there. Fortunately, Cranor had disregarded Garfield's instructions to move toward Prestonburg across the enemy's line of retreat. Mistaking the enemy's retreat for an advance, Cranor had decided to join the main Union column instead. If Marshall had been trapped according to plan, he would have had to stand and fight, resulting in a loss of life for both sides. The way it had worked out, Garfield had halted the rebel advance without firing a single shot. Cranor's arrival was good timing because Bolles' cavalry was leaving. Now for the first time in the campaign, the entire 18th Brigade was together.

On the night of January 8, the Confederates moved 18 miles farther south on the west fork of the river near the town of Prestonburg. They took up a defensive position behind two parallel creeks; the first was Abbott's Creek, and the second, Middle Creek. If they attacked, Union troops would have to cross both creeks under fire.

Pursuing the Enemy

Although Garfield was well aware that his men needed rest, he was impatient to pursue Marshall. Any delay would allow the Confederate general to slip away from him again. So, at noon on January 9, Garfield assembled all of his men who were fit to march (about 1,100) and set out to catch the enemy.

Garfield's men moved through sleet and rain up and down the mountainous terrain, under a hail of snipers' shots. Shortly before dark, tired and chilled, the soldiers reached a hilltop that looked down on Abbott's Creek. Scouts reported that Marshall's force was just ahead behind Middle Creek. Because the enemy was so close, the Union soldiers could not make fires to warm themselves. The weary men, pelted by icy rain, bedded down in their greatcoats and tried to sleep. They got very little rest. Garfield woke them at three o'clock in the morning, and soon they were marching again through deep mud in a dense fog. Around noon, Garfield discovered that he had stumbled upon the enemy's main body of troops. He promptly sent a messenger to Colonel Sheldon asking for reinforcements.

The Battle Is Joined

Garfield surveyed his position. Middle Creek ran through a deep, twisting valley which at times broadened into an open stretch of level land. The hill Garfield's troops had just rounded commanded one end of such a plain. Half a mile across the valley, Confederate troops were dug in behind a steep ridge. Garfield sent two companies up the slope of the hill on his side of the valley to clear out any southerners who might be there. Then he ordered the rest of his troops to march around and around the bottom of the hill. Garfield hoped the drill would give the Confederates an exaggerated idea of his forces. The ruse worked. Marshall later said he was sure that Garfield had at least 5,000 men.

When his scouts reported the hill unoccupied, Garfield stood atop a peak called Grave Yard Point and directed the attack. While Confederate shells screamed overhead, his soldiers charged over the plain and toward the ridge that concealed Marshall's men. The fight went on all day as the Union men struggled to get up the narrow ridge. Garfield desperately needed his reinforcements. When they were sighted in the distance, it brought a cheer from his weary soldiers. However, by the time Sheldon's men reached the bottom of the hill, it was too dark to fight. Garfield recalled his troops, planning to continue the battle in the morning. But the next day he found that Marshall had evacuated the ridge during the night. The Battle of Middle Creek was over. The Union had lost three men and 21 were wounded. It was not a fierce battle, but it was a satisfactory victory and earned Colonel James A. Garfield the reputation of being a fighting man.

A Proud Colonel

Marshall's retreat soon took his troops out of the entire region of eastern Kentucky. There was only one small force left guarding a pass called Pound Gap. Garfield knew the Confederate Army was headed for Virginia, but he did not have enough men to follow Marshall into his own territory. Instead, on January 11, Garfield took possession of Prestonburg. Finding that the rebels had ransacked the town, he had to fall back to Paintsville. Marshall, misinterpreting the move, said the Union had been "well whipped" and claimed victory at Middle Creek.

Garfield may or may not have won the battle, but he had accomplished what he had set out to do. The Confederate drive into the Union flank had been pushed back, and General Buell's position was no longer threatened. Union Commander-in-Chief General George McClellan thanked Garfield for his "handsome achievement." And Buell congratulated him for showing "the highest qualities of a soldier—perseverance and courage."

Colonel James A. Garfield told his troops proudly, ". . . I greet you as brave men. Our common country will not forget you. She will not forget the sacred dead who fell beside you nor those of your comrades who won scars of honor on the field." As winter settled in, there was no doubt among Garfield's weary soldiers that they had been victorious.

Chapter 5

Waiting at the Capital

After the Battle of Middle Creek, victory-starved Union newspapers hailed James A. Garfield as a hero. He was portrayed as a rugged volunteer colonel who had outfoxed a professional soldier. Garfield's friends in Ohio took advantage of the publicity and worked for his promotion to brigadier general. Insisting that he had only done his duty, Garfield said he was not looking for a promotion and would do nothing to get one. Yet he was surely not surprised when, in March of 1862, he was made a brigadier general. The date given for his promotion was January 10, 1862 — the day on which he had fought at Middle Creek.

GENERAL GARFIELD MOVES ON

Marshall left a small force at Pound Gap to guard the entrance to the Virginia territory. The ragged garrison often raided the Kentucky countryside for food and supplies, terrorizing the people there. News of killings and barn burnings reached Garfield at Piketon (now Pikeville), the headquarters of the 18th Brigade, about 50 miles northeast of Pound Gap. Despite a flood and an epidemic of disease that had depleted his forces, Garfield planned to smash the Confederate garrison.

He rode out toward Pound Gap on March 14 with a force of 600 infantry and 100 cavalrymen. When he arrived, Garfield sent his cavalry up the main road toward the pass. At the same time, he and his 600 infantrymen were to climb an unguarded rear mountain path, surprise the Confederates, and cut off their retreat. It was Garfield's favorite plan, but it had never worked and would not now.

Because of a blinding snowstorm, Garfield's infantry took the wrong path. Before they reached their destination, the cavalry began to shoot. Forewarned, the Confederates hastily retreated into Virginia territory. The cavalry started after them, but they had to turn back because of the storm. This minor campaign was the last of Garfield's exploits as commander of the 18th Brigade. Returning to headquarters, he found orders for his regiment to leave Sandy Valley and join General Buell in Louisville.

Union Victories

While Garfield had been pursuing General Marshall's forces, other Union commanders were also defeating the enemy. The victories of General George H. Thomas at Mill Springs and General Ulysses S. Grant at Forts Henry and Donelson had opened the way to Nashville, Tennessee, and beyond. The southern troops had been forced out of central Tennessee, and Confederate General Pierre Beauregard and his forces were now gathered at Corinth, Mississippi. Just 20 miles to the north, General Grant was at a dock called Pittsburg Landing awaiting reinforcements from General Buell in order to attack Beauregard.

When Garfield and his regiment reached Louisville, it was the middle of the night, and Buell had gone ahead with the main body of troops to meet Grant. He had left orders for Garfield to turn over command of the 42nd to Sheldon and Pardee (Garfield had recommended them for promotions) and join him immediately on the road to Pittsburg Landing. Stunned by the orders to leave his boys of the 42nd, Garfield said a quick, emotional good-bye to Sheldon and Pardee. He could not bear to say farewell to his troops. Later he wrote, "It seemed like leaving all in the army that I loved or that loved me."

After riding all night on a fast-trotting horse, Garfield caught up with Buell near Columbia, Tennessee. On April 4, 1862, he took command of the 20th Brigade, Sixth Division of the Army of the Ohio. There were four regiments in his command, the 64th and 65th Ohio, the 13th Michigan, and the 51st Indiana, none of which had yet seen action. That evening, the bands welcomed Garfield with a concert. Yet he missed his old regiment. "No matter what other regiments may be to me," he said, "I mourn like a bereaved lover for my dear old 42nd."

THE BATTLE OF SHILOH

While the bands played for their new commander, the southerners were planning a surprise for the Union soldiers. At dawn on the morning of April 6, 1862, the full Confederate Army attacked a section of the Union Army camped between Pittsburg Landing and a little meetinghouse called Shiloh Church in southwestern Tennessee. It was one of the bloodiest battles of the Civil War. At first it looked as if the Confederates would win. Finally, they were driven off by a combination of Union gunboats (which kept supplies from reaching the Confederates) and the vanguard of Buell's army. General Garfield's 20th Brigade arrived at Shiloh on the second day, when the battle was almost over. Except for a brief skirmish with the enemy cavalry as they retreated toward Corinth, his men saw little action.

After 68 continuous hours of duty, Garfield was very tired and came down with a bad case of dysentery (an intestinal disorder). He had not fully recovered when, at the end of April, the Union Army of over 100,000 men moved out toward Corinth. General Henry Wager Halleck, commander of all Union forces in the West, took charge personally. Although Corinth was less then 20 miles from the Shiloh battleground, "Old Brains," as his troops called Halleck, took his time getting there. Being cautious, he ordered his men to build fortifications every time they stopped.

The Enemy Escapes

Garfield yearned for action. He hated the bridge and road building, and the snail's pace at which they were moving. At last all of Halleck's fortifications were completed and all heavy seige guns were in place. Still he did not order an attack on Corinth. Instead, 10 more days were spent shooting at enemy outposts.

There was sporadic resistance from the Confederates until finally they did not fire back at all. When Halleck's scouts brought word that the southern forces had evacuated Corinth, Garfield was furious. Two months of hard work and they had let the enemy slip away again. "I am nearly disheartened at the way in which the war is conducted here . . . " he wrote.

General McClellan had moved the Army of the Potomac to Virginia and was now confronting Richmond. Admiral David G. Farragut had captured New Orleans, opening up the lower Mississippi as far as Port Hudson. If Halleck had fought Beauregard at Corinth, the Union could have destroyed the Confederates in the West, possibly ending the war at that point.

BACK TO POLITICS

Garfield blamed the sad state of affairs on West Point officers, whom he believed did not want to win the war because it might mean the end of slavery. Slavery was the cause of the war, he reasoned, and only the end of slavery could bring peace.

Deciding that the ballot box was the only way to solve the slavery question, Garfield began to think about returning to politics. The 19th Ohio Congressional District at Hiram had recently been redistricted. He had received many letters asking him to be the new district's Republican candidate for the U.S. House of Representatives. Harry Rhodes wrote Garfield that if he resigned his commission and came home to campaign, he would have an excellent chance to win.

Garfield was tempted. Military life was losing its appeal. He did not like his commanders, his jobs, or the uncouth men of the regular army who chewed tobacco and swore. Being in Hiram with his wife and daughter held much more appeal. Garfield answered Rhodes that he would rather be in Congress than in the Army. If the voters should call on him to serve, he would be pleased to do so. But he would not seek the nomination. Rhodes, Harmon Austin, and other political backers knew Garfield meant he was willing to run. They immediately started a Garfield-for-Congress movement.

The Turchin Incident

In July 1862, Garfield had several more severe dysentery attacks. Despite his illness, however, he spent most of the month presiding over the court-martial of Colonel John Basil Turchin. Turchin was a Russian-born Union cavalry officer. He had been commander of a unit that had attacked the town of Athens, Alabama, in retaliation for the murder of one of his men. Generals Halleck and Buell brought Turchin to trial because he had allowed his soldiers to rape and pillage civilians.

At first Garfield was horrified at the crimes Turchin was accused of. Yet as the trial progressed, he became convinced that Turchin was guilty of nothing but trying to teach the southerners that treason was a crime. He was the only officer, though, who sided with the Russian. Turchin was convicted and dismissed from the service.

During the trial, Garfield became so ill he could not sit up. Refusing to quit, he finished conducting the trial from a stretcher. As soon as it was over, Garfield was relieved of his command and sent home on sick leave. It was almost a year since he had joined the Army.

Nominated for Congress

In early August, when Garfield reached Hiram, Crete and Trot were living with Crete's parents. Garfield took his family to a secluded farmhouse at nearby Howland Springs. A few weeks of warmth and intimacy in their little hideaway was the turning point in the Garfields four years of marriage. James fell deeply in love with his wife. This restless, moody man, who still kept up friendships with Rebecca Selleck and other women, became a devoted if thoughtless husband. He often asked Crete to be patient with him, which she certainly was. As the years went by, the Garfields came to believe that they had an ideal marriage.

On September 2, 1862, while Garfield was still at Howland Springs, the district Republican convention met at Garrettsville, Ohio. Although Garfield later boasted, "I had not lifted a finger nor made a move in my own behalf," his backers fought hard for his nomination for Congress. The incumbent, John Hutchins, did not want to give up his post. On the first several ballots, Hutchins and Garfield were nearly tied. Not until the eighth ballot did Garfield win the nomination—78 votes to 71 for Hutchins. Although election day was a month away, a Republican nominee in Garfield's district was practically assured of being elected.

RETURN TO DUTY

Meanwhile, the war was going badly that summer for the Union Army. The Confederates, with their forces still intact, were in control of both the western and eastern fronts. Confederate General Braxton Bragg's armies marched up through Tennessee into Kentucky, forcing Buell to retreat to defend Louisville and Cincinnati. The end of August brought another Union defeat at the Second Battle of Bull Run. Then, in the first week of September, Confederate General Robert E. Lee and his army crossed the Potomac into Maryland.

Shortly after Garfield was nominated for Congress, he received orders from Secretary of War Edwin Stanton. He was to report to Washington for assignment as soon as he was able. If Garfield was elected, the first congressional session of his term would not be until December of 1863. That meant he still had more than a year of military service ahead. Besides, it had been rumored that he was to receive an important command.

Garfield was feeling much stronger now and was eager to return to active duty after his long rest. On September 16, he said good-bye to his family, left his friends to run his congressional campaign, and went to Washington. He reached the capital just after Lee was defeated at the Battle of Antietam and driven back into Virginia.

Seeking a Command

Arriving in Washington, General James Garfield found a shabby, dirty, capital city filled with suspicion and fear. Its half-finished buildings and monuments stood in silent testimony of a country at war. Thousands of temporary huts occupied by blacks reminded Garfield that only a few years before slaves were bought and sold in the District of Columbia.

Washington was overrun with soldiers. Over 250,000 men were camped in the area. Many bivouacked (camped out) on the steps of the Treasury Building or on the floor of the Capitol rotunda. There were so many officers in the streets that a story was going around about a boy who threw a stone at a dog and hit three brigadier generals instead. It did not take Garfield long to discover he was just one more unemployed brigadier general looking for a combat command. Lucky for him, though, he was invited to stay at the home of Secretary of the Treasury Salmon P. Chase, and he soon became Chase's protege.

On Garfield's first day in Washington, he met with Secretary of War Stanton. Their meeting was cordial, but Stanton told Garfield he had no independent command available just then. Confiding that it would be difficult to find a post where Garfield would not be surrounded by the West Pointers he detested, the secretary offered him command of western Virginia. Garfield declined. Week after week, he stayed on in Washington, keeping after Stanton for a more prestigious assignment. Several possible posts were discussed, but nothing ever materialized.

ELECTION TO CONGRESS

During his stay in the capital, Secretary Chase, an ardent antislavery man, greatly influenced Garfield's thinking. Although Chase was a member of Lincoln's Cabinet, he often criticized the President for being a weak leader. Garfield supported this criticism wholeheartedly. Chase and his friends, the anti-Lincoln Republican radicals of Congress, also criticized Buell and Halleck for the way they had conducted the war. They wanted vengeance against the South, and the more the better.

Then, on September 22, 1862, Abraham Lincoln issued his Emancipation Proclamation, declaring all slaves in districts or states in rebellion against the United States forever free—to take effect on the first of January. Garfield begrudgingly recognized the proclamation as an effective political maneuver. He wrote home that it was a strange moment in history "when a second-rate Illinois lawyer is the instrument to utter words which shall form an epoch memorable in future ages."

In October, Garfield received news of his election to the House of Representatives. He won by an overwhelming margin—13,288 votes to 6,763 for his opponent, D. B. Woods. However, soon after the election, he was criticized by the people at home for his long stay in Washington. He had promised to lead a brigade until his term in Congress began. And the War Department kept telling him that an assignment was imminent. When he did not receive one, he became so frustrated that his dark mood returned. In mid-November, realizing that he had stayed too long at the Chase home, Garfield moved into a boardinghouse on Pennsylvania Avenue.

General Porter's Trial

Meanwhile, Garfield was appointed to be a judge at the court-martial of Major General Fitz-John Porter. The general, a close friend of General George McClellan, was accused of disobedience of orders at the Second Battle of Bull Run. Political enemies charged that professional army officers such as General McClellan and General John Pope (whose army was supposed to take Richmond but retreated instead) were either unable or unwilling to wage all-out war against the Confederacy.

Although it had been bad luck and bad judgment on the part of many men, Pope blamed his losses on General Porter for disobeying orders. Thus Porter became the political scapegoat for all the recent Union defeats. On January 10, 1863, he was found guilty and was dishonorably discharged from the service. (The general fought the verdict for two decades, and it was eventually reversed.)

THE ARMY OF THE CUMBERLAND

Four days after Porter's trial ended, Garfield's long-awaited assignment finally came through. He was ordered to report to General William Starke Rosecrans, who had replaced Buell as commander of the Army of the Cumberland (the new name for the Army of Ohio). Although Rosecrans was a West Point man, Garfield had a great deal of respect for him. He had proved to be a bold leader with strong antislavery convictions.

There were vacancies in the general's high command. Because Rosecrans and Chase were friends, Garfield hoped Chase would use his influence to get him a division. Then, at last, he would win acclaim on the battlefield.

On his way to the front, Garfield stopped in Hiram. Crete and little Trot were delighted to see him. They lived in a small, rented two-story house across from the Eclectic campus. During his short visit Garfield arranged to buy the house for $825. He also paid for additions and repairs.

Chief of Staff

On January 25, 1863, Brigadier General James Garfield, accompanied by a squad of cavalry, reached Murfreesboro, Tennessee, headquarters of General Rosecrans. "Old Rosy" (Rosecrans' nickname) had occupied Murfreesboro as the result of a narrowly won battle at Stone's River. Because of the recent numerous Union defeats, winning this battle had earned Rosecrans the reputation of being a bold fighter. However, two of his divisions lost their commanders in the heavy fighting at Stone's River. General Rosecrans' chief of staff had also been killed in the battle.

Rosecrans kept Garfield at his headquarters for three weeks discussing military affairs, as well as moral and theological matters. They became such good friends that Rosecrans seemed reluctant to assign James to active duty. Garfield was getting more impatient every day. Finally, in the middle of February, Rosecrans offered him the post of chief of staff of the Army of the Cumberland.

Garfield was highly complimented. As chief of staff, he would become the general's closest advisor and confidant. But would it be good politics to tie his future to one general? He had seen enough maneuvering in Washington to know that it did not take much for top generals to be dismissed.

Garfield could not make up his mind whether to accept the assignment. If he declined the post, he might be given a division. Then, at the end of February, Rosecrans decided for him. He assigned Garfield to duty as his chief of staff.

Although Rosecrans was a tireless, energetic commander, he was not an easy man to work for. Occasionally, he would explode with anger over some matter, and it was difficult to calm him down. Garfield's main duty was to help the general keep his army running smoothly. He spent most of his time at headquarters, where he would sit on a high stool at a small pine desk issuing orders in Rosecrans' name. They had to be delivered to 16 separate commands. Many of the generals in the Army of the Cumberland liked Garfield, but some resented his influence over Rosecrans. Yet for the most part, Garfield was happy with his job.

Chapter 6

The General's Friend

After the battle at Stone's River in early 1863, Confederate General Braxton Bragg had retreated to Tullahoma, Tennessee. It was 35 miles southeast of Murfreesboro, where Rosecrans' army was stationed. Bragg's army was not as large as the Army of the Cumberland, but his cavalry was superior in quality and quantity. Secretary of War Stanton ordered Rosecrans to attack Tullahoma and clean out the Confederates. Rosecrans sent word back to Stanton that his army was not prepared. He asked the War Department first for more men, then more horses, food, and medicine, until Stanton lost patience and refused further requests. The long wait was driving Garfield mad. As far as he was concerned, the Army of the Cumberland had been ready to move way back in March.

ROSECRANS' DOWNFALL

Finally, at the beginning of June, Rosecrans said he was ready. Yet on June 8, the designated date of departure, he hesitated again and sent a memo to his commanders asking their advice about the attack. For different reasons, each of those polled was against an immediate advance. Garfield could not believe it. He sent Rosecrans a long letter on the subject, closing with nine arguments to persuade him to move against the enemy immediately. Courageously, Garfield included a subtle reminder to Rosecrans that he could be replaced by a more aggressive commander. The general did not always take Garfield's advice, but this time he did.

It was June 24, during a violent storm, when the Army of the Cumberland finally moved out of Murfreesboro. If they had attacked two weeks earlier, they would have fought in clear weather. Nevertheless, once Old Rosy was in the field, he proved to be a bold and skillful commander. In nine days of hard fighting, he outflanked the Confederates at Shelbyville and Tullahoma, forcing Bragg to retreat.

Bragg's army fled across the mountains and the Tennessee River to Chattanooga. Because of the storm, which had continued throughout the entire campaign, Union troops were unable to go after Bragg and deliver the decisive blow. Yet Rosecrans considered the battle to be a great victory. He complimented his staff and had special praise for James Garfield. "I feel much indebted to him, for both counsel and assistance in the administration of this army," he said. "Garfield possesses the instincts and energy of a great commander."

A Disappointed Secretary

On July 4, at about the time that Lee's army was defeated at Gettysburg and Vicksburg surrendered to Grant, Rosecrans reported to Stanton that he had chased the Confederates from eastern Tennessee. However, because of the greater victories at Gettysburg and Vicksburg, Rosecrans' small campaign received very little notice from the press and Washington authorities.

In fact, Stanton was disappointed that Rosecrans had let Bragg get away. He sent the general a telegram which said, "You and your noble army now have the chance to give the finishing blow to the rebellion. Will you neglect the chance?" Rosecrans replied that he would prefer a joint offensive against Bragg where Grant's army would support the Army of the Cumberland on its right flank. Although it was not a bad idea, it was turned down in Washington.

A Loss of Confidence

Again Rosecrans delayed the offensive, claiming to need reinforcements—especially cavalry. Garfield did not agree with his commander. When Rosecrans sent a general to Washington to insist on more cavalry, it was the last straw for Garfield. He had a great deal of affection for Rosecrans but he was losing confidence in his military judgment.

On July 27, Garfield poured out his disappointment in a long, confidential letter to Secretary Chase. He told Chase that he was dissatisfied with the slow progress that Rosecrans' army had made since the battle of Stone's River. It was extremely urgent, Garfield said, for the army to push on before Bragg received replacements from Mississippi.

Garfield said he was writing the letter in sorrow because he had only the highest admiration for Rosecrans. There is no question that as Rosecrans' chief of staff Garfield was wrong to write to a member of the government. Yet he did it believing he was performing a painful but necessary duty. When Chase showed Garfield's letter to Stanton, the secretary of war became angry with Rosecrans. He denied the general any reinforcements and ordered the Army of the Cumberland to advance immediately.

Old Rosy Retreats

Prodded by Garfield and the War Department, Rosecrans moved against Bragg in mid-August. On September 10, while awaiting reinforcements, Bragg pulled back, and Rosecrans

occupied Chattanooga. Old Rosy was sure his superior gener-
alship had caused Bragg's army to flee in confusion to Rome,
Georgia.

At his headquarters in Chattanooga, scouts brought word
to General Rosecrans that Bragg's army might not be in retreat; rather, they seemed to be preparing to attack. Rosecrans was worried and confided his concern to Charles A.
Dana, second assistant secretary of war, who had just arrived
in Chattanooga. Rosecrans liked Dana and trusted him, but
the secretary was not his friend. He was there to spy on Rosecrans for the War Department.

A few days later, although the mountains hid Bragg's position, positive proof reached General Rosecrans that the
enemy was getting ready to fight. He quickly assembled his
army at Chickamauga Creek, a wooded area 12 miles south
of Chattanooga. On September 19, Bragg attacked. After a
day of fierce fighting, both armies were still in the field. Then,
as Garfield had feared, two fresh battle-tested divisions arrived to reinforce the enemy. Now the Confederates had more
men than the Union.

The next morning, a gap was reported in the center of
the Union line. Rosecrans ordered troops from another area
to close the gap. The report was wrong; a division had been
there all the time. But by pulling some of his troops out of
line, Rosecrans had actually created a gap where there had
been none. Taking advantage of the breach, the Confederates attacked. They split the Union Army, causing a rout at
its right and center. Rosecrans and his officers tried their best
to restore order, but it was impossible.

The Union soldiers fled the battlefield, stampeding up
Dry Valley Road toward Rossville. When Rosecrans and his
staff tried to join General George Thomas on the left, enemy
columns blocked them. So they, too, were forced to retreat
up Dry Valley Road. Under heavy musketfire, they rode past

The General's Friend   61

running soldiers, scared horses, and abandoned artillery. Rosecrans was silent in defeat. At times he was so deep in thought he seemed oblivious to what was going on.

The information reaching the Union generals seemed to indicate the collapse of Rosecrans' entire army. Yet, they heard firing from the direction of General Thomas' lines. To Garfield, it sounded as if Thomas was still in the fight. He asked Rosecrans for permission to find Thomas' army and see what was happening on the left. Rosecrans, who thought the firing was simply scattered volleys from his retreating army, listlessly gave his approval.

Bidding Garfield a sad good-bye, Rosecrans continued on. His aim was to get to Chattanooga as soon as possible and prepare to defend the city. The retreat to Chattanooga destroyed Rosecrans' military career. For the rest of his life, he kept trying to explain why he had left the battlefield at Chickamauga.

A Dangerous Mission

While Rosecrans headed north, Garfield, with a staff officer and two orderlies, rode toward the left end of the Union Army. In order to get through, the tiny party had to cut across open country. They had almost reached their destination when Confederate troops began firing at them. Garfield got to the Union lines unharmed, but one of his orderlies was killed, and Garfield's horse was wounded. Yet for Garfield it was a "glorious moment." Joining General Thomas, still fighting, separated Garfield from General Rosecrans and defeat. And in later years, his ride was glorified as an heroic epic.

Although outnumbered and surrounded, General Thomas' troops held off the Confederate advance, enabling the rest of Rosecrans' army to retreat safely to Chattanooga. Because of Thomas' courageous stand, he earned the name "The Rock of Chickamauga."

Trapped in Chattanooga

Shortly after the Battle of Chickamauga, the entire Army of the Cumberland (including Generals Garfield and Thomas) was assembled in Chattanooga. Against Garfield's advice, Rosecrans had evacuated Lookout Mountain, a high point in Chattanooga that guarded the main route to the Union supply depot at Bridgeport on the Tennessee River. Garfield had warned Rosecrans that if they were cut off from their supplies, the Union could lose the entire Tennessee campaign. On September 23, 1863, Garfield sent a desperate telegram to Chase. Pleading for 25,000 men to be sent to Bridgeport within 10 days, he hoped to secure middle Tennessee in case of a disaster at Chattanooga.

In response to Garfield's telegram, Secretary Stanton called an emergency midnight meeting at the War Department. Even President Lincoln attended. Orders were approved to send two veteran corps of the Army of the Potomac to aid Rosecrans. By some miracle, all red tape was slashed, and with the cooperation of the nation's leading railroad men, seven days later over 20,000 fully equipped soldiers began arriving in Bridgeport.

But the battle was not yet won. In early October, the Confederates did indeed cut off the Union supply lines. As Garfield had predicted, it had been a mistake to evacuate Lookout Mountain. Soldiers went on short rations and animals died for lack of food as Rosecrans worked on a plan to bring supplies into Chattanooga by boat. Refusing to take any of the blame himself, Rosecrans lashed out at mistakes made by Stanton, Halleck, and even his own officers. Garfield felt sorry for his friend and tried to calm him down.

When officials came out from Washington to investigate the situation, the officers trapped in Chattanooga needed someone to blame. Because they had left the battlefield, Generals Crittenden and McCook became scapegoats. That put Rosecrans in an awkward position, for he, too, had left the battlefield.

Relieved of Duty

Garfield was uneasy with the charges and countercharges being flung about the officers' quarters. Although he liked Rosecrans and thought he was an honorable and courageous man, he could see that his days as commander of the Army of the Cumberland were numbered. Luckily, Garfield did not have to take sides. Just then, he received orders to report to Washington.

Thus it was that on October 15, 1863, General Rosecrans relieved James Garfield of his military duties as chief of staff and sent him off to the nation's capital with the official report of the Battle of Chickamauga, which Garfield was to deliver to the War Department. Before he left, General Thomas told Garfield to set matters right for Rosecrans in Washington because Rosecrans had been unjustly attacked.

Meanwhile, Secretary of War Stanton was having an important meeting with General Grant to discuss a change in command for the Army of the Cumberland. Garfield found out about the meeting on October 19, when he was in Nashville. Although he tried to get in touch with Rosecrans to warn him, it was too late. It had already been decided that Grant would assume command of the new Military division of the Mississippi. Moreover, Grant had chosen Thomas to replace Rosecrans as commander of the Army of the Cumberland, which was now part of Grant's new command.

OFF TO CONGRESS

A few days later, Garfield was in Louisville for a meeting with Stanton. Being an expert trial lawyer, Stanton skillfully questioned Garfield about Rosecrans' conduct at Chickamauga. When it was over, the secretary decided that Garfield's testimony confirmed the worst reports he had received from Charles Dana, the War Department spy.

After the meeting, Garfield spent a few days in Cincinnati and Hiram. The following week, he delivered Rosecrans' papers to General Halleck and President Lincoln. In his interviews, Garfield always had a kind word for Rosecrans. When he heard that Rosecrans had been assigned to fight guerrillas in Missouri, he wrote to the stunned and broken commander. His letters were those of a good friend shocked by the "great wrong" done to him. Garfield said, "You are a power among the people, which no action of the War Department can destroy." He kept up a friendship with Rosecrans that lasted for 17 years.

An Angry Friend

As Garfield became politically more prominent, stories began to be circulated that he had been disloyal to Rosecrans while serving as his chief of staff. The leading instigator of these reports was Dana, who later became editor of the *New York Sun*. Dana alleged that Garfield had Rosecrans ousted from his command by writing the letter to Chase from Chattanooga. The truth was that most of Stanton's information that had helped to oust Rosecrans had come from Dana himself.

In 1880, because of Dana's articles, Rosecrans wrote an angry letter to Garfield attacking him on various charges. Garfield answered with an unqualified denial that he had ever been an unfaithful friend. It is now believed that although

Garfield had the highest regard for Rosecrans as a friend (and he later proved it), he thought that it was for the good of the nation that Rosecrans be removed as commander of the Army of the Cumberland.

In November, Garfield went to the White House to ask President Lincoln's advice about whether to continue in military service or take his seat in Congress. While there, he learned that he had been promoted to major general dating from the Battle of Chickamauga. Lincoln convinced Garfield that he needed a military man in Congress, someone who understood army affairs. So Garfield chose Congress.

Sad Times in Hiram

Garfield returned to Hiram to await the opening of Congress and see his new son, Harry, named for Harry Rhodes. Joy over the boy's birth soon turned to sorrow when their beloved 3½-year-old Trot came down with a bad case of diphtheria (a bacterial disease). She died on December 1, 1863, leaving her parents grief-stricken. Right after the funeral, seven-week-old Harry showed the same horrible symptoms. Garfield delayed his return to Washington until the baby's fever broke. Then, lonely and heavy-hearted, he left for the capital and settled in a boardinghouse on Pennsylvania Avenue.

On December 6, just before the 38th Congress opened, Major General James Garfield discarded his uniform and became Representative James Garfield of Ohio. He took his seat in the House of Representatives that he would hold for the next 17 years.

Chapter 7

Congressman Garfield

On December 7, 1863, while dressing to attend the opening session of Congress, Garfield was told to wear a pistol under his new civilian suit. It was for protection in the event the Democrats tried to capture the organization of the House of Representatives. Fortunately, everything went smoothly and he did not need it.

THE 38TH CONGRESS

The 183 representatives of the 38th Congress met in a room called the Hall of the House in the south wing of the Capitol. Although newly decorated, the tremendous, windowless room was not very comfortable. Because of its poor lighting and ventilation, Garfield complained that his skull and brain were roasting. Only committee chairmen had offices; representatives had to conduct business from their congressional seats or at their boardinghouses.

House members paid little attention to those who stood up to speak, but that did not bother Garfield. Although he was a first-term congressman, he talked whenever and as much as he wanted. In contrast to the new brief style of speaking of the other House members, Garfield's preacher-like oratory was quite long-winded. Nevertheless, he was one of the few members of Congress whose booming voice could get the legislators' attention and keep it.

The Republican (Union) Party was the majority party in the 38th Congress. Its members were loosely held together by their support of the war. On the Democratic side of the aisle, there were many empty seats belonging to the seceded states. Democrats in the House found themselves in a predicament. If they opposed the war, they would be called traitors. If they supported the war—and most did—they would lose their Democratic identity. There was also a powerful radical Republican wing. The leaders were Thaddeus Stevens of Pennsylvania, Robert C. Schenck of Ohio, who was chairman of the Military Affairs Committee, and Henry Winter Davis of Maryland.

The Military Affairs Committee

Because of his war experience, James Garfield was given an important and demanding assignment on the Military Affairs Committee. Chairman Schenck took the new congressman under his wing. Together they worked to get a draft law through Congress that would help Lincoln maintain the Union Army.

The two men had a lot in common. Both were from Ohio, and both were generals and radical Republicans. So when Schenck asked Garfield, who was still mourning the death of his little daughter, to board with him, the lonely young congressman was delighted. A deluge of army business soon turned their rooms into a "second army headquarters."

LINCOLN'S RE-ELECTION

In his message to Congress in December 1863, President Lincoln proposed a simple plan for the reconstruction of the South after the war. Eleven states had left the Union. In order to be readmitted, 10 percent of the voters of a seceded state had to take an oath to support the U.S. Constitution. They also had to accept emancipation of the slaves. The President's plan pleased very few congressmen. Democrats countered with their own plan for an immediate end of the war and recognition of the Confederacy. Garfield and the other radical members of Congress sneered at the Democrats, and they criticized Lincoln for not punishing the South. Poking fun at the President for being soft on the South became a popular game in Washington.

In the spring of 1864, the radical Republicans started a Chase-for-President movement. Garfield would have liked his friend Salmon Chase to become President, but the voters back in Hiram preferred Lincoln. So Garfield convinced Chase not to run and reluctantly announced his support of Abraham Lincoln.

About that time, Chase was accused of fraud and treason in conducting the affairs of the Treasury Department. Garfield was appointed chairman of a committee to investigate the charges, so it was not surprising that Chase was found innocent. Later, Garfield accused Lincoln of being behind the attack on Chase. Although Lincoln denied it, Garfield was sorry he had endorsed the President for re-election. But with the Republican National Convention only a few weeks away, it was too late to do anything about it.

In June 1864, Lincoln was renominated with Andrew Johnson, former governor of Tennessee (and friend of Garfield's), as his Vice-President. Garfield did not think the Republican ticket had a chance to win.

The Wade-Davis Manifesto

Garfield was wrong. Although he and his radical friends criticized the President and thought they could run the country better than he did, the people of the United States were solidly behind Lincoln. But despite Lincoln's popularity, the radicals managed to push a measure through Congress called the Wade-Davis bill. It was devised so that after the war, reconstruction would be under congressional rather than executive control. Of course, Lincoln did not sign the bill, and the radicals were furious. Senator Ben Wade and Representative Henry Davis then wrote a manifesto against Lincoln that was published in the *New York Tribune.* It was terribly disrespectful to the President and created an uproar throughout the nation.

Many thought Garfield had written the manifesto. He was up for re-election in his own district, and the state Republican convention questioned him about it. When Garfield saw that the manifesto could cost him his seat in Congress, he said angrily, "I am not a piece of merchandise subject to their caprices and wishes." He told his constituents honestly that Lincoln was not his first choice for President. And although he did not write the manifesto, he believed in it. If they sent him back to Congress, he said, he must go as a free man. He ended by saying, "When you are unwilling to grant me my freedom of opinion to the highest degree I have no longer any desire to represent you."

With those words, Garfield walked out of the convention hall. When he reached the door, he heard a great roar. The convention was shouting its approval of Garfield's independent stand. Although Wade and Davis were later censured by the convention, Garfield was renominated—and on his own terms. He won the election by a large margin.

After the campaign, Crete pointed out to her husband

that she had seen very little of him in the almost five years they had been married. Therefore, in December 1864, when he returned to Washington for the second session of the 38th Congress, Garfield rented quarters for his growing family. It now included a new son, James Rudolph. From then on, although he could barely afford it, his family lived with him whenever he was in Washington.

A NEW ERA

On April 14, 1865, Garfield was in New York on business. Next morning he heard that President Lincoln had been shot at Ford's Theatre in Washington the evening before. He was shocked. Now Garfield had nothing but praise for the man he had criticized so often in the past. "They slew the noblest and gentlest heart that ever put down a rebellion upon this earth," he said.

That spring, the Civil War ended in victory for the Union, and reconstruction began a new era for the United States. Andrew Johnson was now President. When the 39th Congress opened in December 1865, there were many questions to be decided. One of the most important was: Should former slaves be given full civil rights immediately, including the right to vote? Garfield believed so. Others disagreed. They argued that most former slaves could not even read or write, so how could they vote? Garfield insisted that, except for the color of their skin, freed slaves were no different from the European immigrants who were flooding the country again. Many of them could not even speak English, let alone read and write. "If an education test were to be given," Garfield said, "let it apply to all alike."

Another question facing the Congress was how to handle the defeated southern states. Garfield wanted former Confederates to show proof that they could be trusted before they were readmitted to the Union. Proof, he said, would be to grant blacks the right to vote.

Role as a Peacemaker

When President Johnson took office, radical Republican leaders thought he held views similar to theirs on many issues. Yet two months after he became President, Johnson issued a series of proclamations showing he intended to follow Lincoln's plan for reconstruction. That meant he was going to readmit the southern states without further conditions. The radicals were horrified and began gearing up for a fight.

Garfield thought he would have a friendly talk with the President and try to smooth things out between him and Congress. After a few meetings, during which they had what Garfield called a "full and free" exchange of views, Garfield was optimistic about Johnson's cooperation. He told his radical friends to be patient and to "treat the President kindly, and without suspicion. . . . "

It was not easy in those emotionally charged days to treat the President kindly. Although Johnson depended on Garfield to act as a mediator in his battle with Congress, he had a bad temper and did many things that widened the breach. On February 1, 1866, Garfield delivered a speech in which he tried hard to find some common ground on which Congress and the President could agree. The speech was applauded, but it could not stop the clash that was coming between President Johnson and Congress.

THE PRESIDENT BATTLES CONGRESS

A few weeks later, the President vetoed a bill to extend the term of the Freedman's Bureau, the only federal agency that dealt with protecting the rights of former slaves. To Garfield, it was as if Johnson had declared war on Congress. He gave up his role as a peacemaker and rejoined the radicals, saying, "The President has left the true men of the country no choice but to fight him, and fight it is."

On February 22, President Johnson stated publicly that several leading radical Republicans were traitors. Soon afterward he vetoed another Freedman's Bureau Act as well as a Civil Rights Act supported by moderate as well as radical Republicans. In a speech at Hagerstown, Maryland, in May, Garfield retaliated by saying that President Johnson had joined the Democrats—the party of rebellion and secession. Garfield the peacemaker had become President Johnson's worst enemy.

Defending "Copperheads"

But James Garfield was a complex man. Back in 1865, he had become involved in an important case defending Indiana copperheads (northerners who sympathized with southerners during the Civil War). Lambdin P. Milligan and two friends had been charged with treason during the war, tried by military courts, and sentenced to be hanged. Later President Johnson commuted their sentences to life imprisonment. When the war was over, Garfield was asked by his law partner to join the attorneys for the defense and work to free the men. Because they had been tried by military courts when civil courts were open, his partner said that their sentences were unconstitutional. The case was to be tried before the U.S. Supreme Court.

Although Garfield knew the people of his district would not like him defending copperheads, he considered it a challenge. For four days and nights he studied the subject. His two-hour plea before the Court cited historical and legal precedents that applied to the case. When the decision was announced in Milligan's favor and the defendants freed, some radicals accused Garfield of betraying them by going over to the Democrats.

Election of 1866

Garfield had not gone over to the Democrats. He was still a Republican and showed it in the crucial congressional election of 1866. When Johnson campaigned vigorously for the election of a Congress that would accept his reconstruction plan, Garfield campaigned just as hard against him. At the outcome, the Republicans held 80 percent of the Senate seats and 75 percent of the seats in the House of Representatives. Most Republicans favored the radical agenda.

BLACK RECONSTRUCTION

Congress had won the right to control reconstruction. It began by dividing the South into military districts. Sometimes two states were combined as one district under the command of a harsh military man. Garfield supported the military districting plan. Under the new laws passed by Congress, southern whites lost their right to vote and hold office. Carpetbaggers (so-called because they carried their belongings in a traveling bag made of carpet fabric) from the North joined with blacks who were often illiterate and took control of municipal governments in the South. After stealing as much money as they could from city treasuries, the carpetbaggers would move on. The blacks they left behind were not only penniless, they also had to live alongside their former masters, who resented those who had been in authority.

Law by law over the President's veto, Congress demolished Johnson's mild reconstruction plan and practically deprived the President of his authority. They forced through measures such as one curbing Johnson's powers so that he could not appoint new Supreme Court justices. The Command of the Army Act of 1867 deprived him of command of the country's armed forces. The way the all-powerful radicals controlled the country was later called, "black reconstruction."

The President fought back. On March 2 he vetoed a bill providing for the indefinite military occupation of the South. Although Congress passed the bill over his veto, radicals could see that as long as Johnson was President they would have to fight him on every issue. Talk of impeachment (removal from office) began.

European Trip

When the congressional session came to a close, Mr. and Mrs. Garfield left for Europe. They sailed on July 13, 1867, on the *City of London* to Liverpool, England. Garfield had dreamed of a sea voyage ever since he had been a sea-struck canal boy. They toured cities in many countries during their 17-week trip, but Rome, Italy, was the emotional high point for Garfield. They returned home in November in time for the next session of Congress.

In December 1867, Garfield voted against a resolution to impeach (bring legal charges of misconduct against) the President of the United States. In February 1868, when new articles of impeachment were drawn, Garfield supported them. But he was away from Washington, trying his second law suit, when the vote was taken. President Johnson came within one vote of losing his office. Garfield was stunned. Accusing Chief Justice Salmon Chase, who presided over the trial, of using his influence to convince senators to vote for acquittal, Garfield broke off their friendship. Actually, there were no constitutional grounds on which to impeach Johnson. The only thing the President was guilty of was fighting against policies which the Republican Party favored.

THE COMMITTEE MAN

Committee memberships were Garfield's life in the House of Representatives. With the end of the war, the Military Affairs Committee had lost its importance. Garfield asked for and was assigned to the Committee on Ways and Means. He served there until he was made chairman of the Military Affairs Committee. But his interest now was in money and finance. In 1869 he was appointed chairman of the Committee on Banking and Currency. Becoming an expert in finance later won Garfield the chairmanship of the Appropriations Committee.

The Black Friday Scandal

It was while serving as chairman of the Banking and Currency Committee that James Garfield won acclaim for investigating one of the worst financial conspiracies in American history. Jim Fiske and Jay Gould, two financiers, tried to corner the gold market (buying gold in such large volume that they could control its price). Cornering is against federal law. Because the conspiracy came to light on Friday, September 24, 1869, it was called the "Black Friday Scandal."

When gold was at its lowest price, Gould bought seven million dollars worth in one day. He hoped that by buying such a large amount he could drive the price back up, sell at a much higher price, and make a lot of money.

In June 1869, Gould and his friends heard President Grant say that the price of gold was too high. They panicked. If the President ordered the Treasury Department to sell gold to bring the price down, they would lose a great deal of money. So they took Grant's brother-in-law, A. R. Corbin, into their scheme, hoping he would use his influence to keep Grant from acting. The President learned about the plot and told Mrs. Grant to warn her brother to get out of the deal. When Corbin reported the warning to Gould, the conspirators secretly sold their gold while the price was still high.

On Friday, September 24, the Treasury Department sold four million dollars of gold. Because gold fell from $160 an ounce to $133 an ounce in 15 minutes, hundreds of speculators were wiped out. Many Wall Street brokerage houses were also ruined. When the House asked for an investigation, Garfield, as chairman of the Committee on Banking and Currency, personally took charge. He managed to attend a private meeting of the Gold Board (those in the business community who controlled the traffic in gold) on Wall Street. Upon leaving the meeting before it was over, he had subpoenas (legal papers requiring a person to appear in court) issued to the men immediately. The conspirators were taken to Washington that very day. Testifying before Congress, Gould, Fiske, and the others admitted their guilt. James Garfield won the public's enthusiastic approval for his prompt action in the Black Friday Scandal.

Garfield was re-elected to Congress eight consecutive times. He was so sure of his seat in the House that in 1869 he sold his house in Hiram and built a home in Washington for his growing family, which now included a daughter, Mary (Mollie). Crete was expecting another baby (Irvin), and in 1872 Abram was born.

Chapter 8

Government Scandals

After Ulysses S. Grant became President in 1869, reconstruction mostly meant maintaining military rule in the South while enforcing the 14th and 15th Amendments. These amendments gave blacks the right to vote and protected them legally. The abolition of slavery had now been accomplished. Another important issue during Grant's administration was when and on what terms home rule was to be returned to the South. Although the war caused many social issues that continued to be problems, they became so complex that Garfield lost interest in them. He began instead to concentrate on other legislative matters.

POSITION ON ISSUES

As chairman of the House Appropriations Committee, Garfield studied what things cost and figured how much money should be allotted to each government project. Working 15 hours a day and sometimes more, he visited offices, hospitals, and schools and watched how the public's money was being spent. Garfield knew what was going on in every department of the rapidly expanding government.

The federal government was also responsible for maintaining adequate and sound currency for the growing economy. After a great deal of study, Garfield concluded that all new money issued by the government be backed by gold in the federal treasury, that notes (dollar bills) be issued only by the national banking system, and that payment of the national debt be made in coin. This was called advocating "sound money."

When it came to the tariff (duty imposed by the government on imported goods), Garfield said, "I am for a protection which leads to ultimate free trade. I am for that free trade which can be only achieved through protection." It was double talk, but Garfield ultimately convinced the protectionists (those who favored high tariffs) that he was not a free trader.

Always interested in education, Garfield favored using money from the sale of public lands to fund education. He was instrumental in establishing the National Department of Education (Bureau of Education). Everyone should be educated, he said, no matter what their skin color or station in life.

As Appropriations Committee chairman, Garfield was an important link between politics and science. Leading scientists came to him for help in getting money from Congress for their work. One scientist named a western mountain Mount Garfield in honor of James Garfield.

Garfield's interest in Indian affairs led him to believe that the Interior Department was doing a poor job of managing the Indians. In December 1868, he introduced a bill to transfer the control of Indian affairs to the War Department. He forced the bill through the House in less than an hour. Although it was killed in the Senate, Garfield reintroduced it every chance he had. He even tried tacking it onto other bills. By the mid-1870s, however, Garfield's views changed. He admitted that civilian agents were doing a good job of handling Indian affairs.

Improving the Census

As chairman of the subcommittee assigned to modernize the government's census-taking procedures, Garfield did an excellent job. He and his committee introduced a census bill that would have broadened the census into a great fact-gathering agency and would have provided valuable information for legislators. Although the bill passed the House, it was rejected in the Senate. Ten years later, many of Garfield's recommendations were included in a bill for the planning of the 1880 census. Sunset Cox, the manager of that bill, gave Garfield full credit for his work. From then on Garfield was called the "father of the modern census."

Garfield's many years of service in the House earned him a great deal of respect. But he was disappointed to see President Grant surround himself with men whom Garfield thought were unfit for government service. Under the "spoils system," the winning political party gave public offices to those who campaigned for its candidates. During Grant's administration, the system was a disgrace. Office seekers haunted congressmen for jobs. Garfield called finding jobs for these people "the most intolerable burden I have to bear." Thus, by 1870 he had become a champion of civil service reform, selecting government workers based on experience and ability rather than political connections.

CREDIT MOBILIER

Three events between September 1872 and April 1874 almost ruined Garfield's reputation. They were the Credit Mobilier scandal, the Salary Grab, and the DeGolyer pavement affair.

After the Civil War, the people of the United States were extremely enthusiastic about railroads. Considering them to be remarkable technological achievements, Congress often gave money and land to help build railroads. One of the most important was the Pacific Railroad (Union Pacific). It linked Chicago and the East with California and the West.

In 1867 there were still 667 miles of Union Pacific Railroad to be completed. Seven of its directors, led by Congressman Oakes Ames, met to discuss how to make the most profit from its construction. Previously, they had bought control of a small Pennsylvania corporation named the Credit Mobilier Company of America. Now they put aside 160 shares of Credit Mobilier stock to be sold at its par (issued value) of $100 a share to congressmen and others who were in a position to help Credit Mobilier get the contract to finish the railroad line. Because the stock was then selling at about double that amount on the open market, all a buyer had to do in order to make a quick profit was to sell. Oakes Ames was put in charge of distributing the stock. Subsequently, Credit Mobilier obtained the contract to build the rest of the line.

Rumors of Fraud

The Union Pacific Railroad was completed on May 10, 1869. Actual cost of the construction ran about $16,000 a mile through flat country and up to $50,000 a mile in mountain areas. When Credit Mobilier presented their bills to Union Pacific, however, they upped the price to $42,000 a mile in flat country and $96,000 a mile in the mountains. The railroad borrowed money and obtained grants from Congress to pay the bills. The seven conspirators split nearly $20 million among themselves.

Rumors of fraud in connection with Credit Mobilier began. The Union Pacific was not just another railroad; it had been heavily subsidized by Congress. If fraud was proven,

it would be a full-fledged national disgrace. Yet nothing further happened until 1872, when Henry S. McComb, a direc-
tor of Credit Mobilier, accused Congressman Ames of keeping
stock for himself that was supposed to have been set aside
for distribution to influential men.

Ames denied the charge. He gave McComb a list of those
to whom he had sold stock at the low rate. The list included
the Vice-President of the United States, Schuyler Colfax;
Speaker of the House James G. Blaine; and James A.
Garfield, chairman of the House Committee on Appropriations. Because McComb did not believe that the people on
the list had actually received the stock, he hired a lawyer to
sue Ames. But when McComb's lawyer warned him that if
the case went to court, many men in high government positions could be ruined. McComb withdrew the case. Nevertheless, he still did not trust Ames. Many letters were exchanged
between the two men, and some of them fell into the hands
of Charles A. Dana of the *New York Sun*, who published the
material.

The Poland Committee Investigation

Although Garfield's name was on Ames' list, he denied all
charges of fraud. He had his own version of the matter. A
few years earlier, when Ames had offered him the Credit
Mobilier stock and he did not have the money to pay for it,
Ames urged him to take it on credit. Garfield did not know
then that Credit Mobilier was connected with the Union
Pacific Railroad or that either of the companies was commit-
ting any wrong-doing. Later, he was paid some money that
he considered to be a loan.

Several years before the scandal came to light, Garfield's

friend, Jeremiah Black (who was also McComb's lawyer), told Garfield what was going on. Garfield immediately returned the money to Ames. In 1872, he continued to deny the charges, hoping the whole mess would soon blow over. It may have, if it had not been for House Speaker Blaine, who insisted on a congressional investigation. A committee was set up, headed by Congressman Luke Poland of Vermont.

Ames' first testimony before the committee supported Garfield's version of what had happened. But later, Ames changed his testimony. Because five years had passed since the original transaction, he said, he had not remembered the facts accurately when he had first testified. However, after checking his records again, he found that dividends had accrued on the 10 shares of Credit Mobilier stock he was holding in Garfield's name. The dividends soon covered the purchase price, and within a few months Garfield owned his shares free and clear. There was even a balance of $329 that Ames paid Garfield. Although Garfield had called the money a loan and had repaid it, Ames insisted it was a dividend on the Credit Mobilier stock.

Because he feared the issue could destroy his political career, Garfield did not testify again. Therefore, the Poland Committee believed Ames' story. For Garfield and Crete, this was a most stressful time. Garfield became depressed and filled with gloom. He was bitterly attacked, not only by Democrats but also by voters in his own district, and forced to make endless explanations and denials.

The Poland Committee report was presented to Congress on February 18, 1873. It recommended that Representative Ames and Representative James Brooks of New York be expelled from the House. But after 10 days of discussion, the members voted only to censure (officially reprimand) the men. When a motion was made to include Garfield and another congressman in the censure, it was not passed.

THE SALARY GRAB

In the last week of February 1873, Garfield found himself involved in another controversy, the Salary Grab. Representative Benjamin Butler, an opponent of Garfield's, introduced an amendment to the General Appropriations Bill to increase the salary of congressmen from $5,000 to $7,500 a year. The increase was to be retroactive, going back to the beginning of the 42nd Congress two years earlier.

Because the reputation of Congress was still reeling from the Credit Mobilier scandal, Garfield knew the Butler amendment would mean trouble. Therefore, he spoke against it, but it passed anyway. Later, after a similar measure passed in the Senate, Garfield once again opposed the bill. Nevertheless, it passed over his objections.

When Ohioans found out about the Salary Grab, it brought Garfield more grief than the Poland Committee report. Farmers of the Western Reserve were having a hard time making ends meet and did not care that Garfield had been against the Butler amendment from the very beginning. As chairman of the Appropriations Committee, he had signed the bill. Therefore, he was a villain. Newspapers denounced him. He was condemned at Republican conventions in three counties of his district and was called upon to resign. Garfield noted bitterly, "They blame me for that vote as if I had been for the increase all the time."

This swift plunge from public favor left Garfield bewildered. He slipped into one of his moods of gloom and doom. "Public life," he said, "is one of the hollowest of all shams."

Fighting Back

Garfield's friends urged him to fight back. But he was so deeply hurt and full of self-pity, he would not. Harmon Austin, Garfield's political manager, told him that if he did not speak out, his silence would be construed as guilt and weakness. Finally, Congressman Garfield was able to see the matter as a lesson in discipline. He decided to fight for his honor and integrity.

The first thing Garfield did was return his share of the salary increase to the Treasury Department. His friends immediately leaked this gesture to the press. Then he wrote long letters to influential constituents and spent many hours devising a pamphlet and an open letter to Republican voters of his district giving his version of the Credit Mobilier affair and the Salary Grab. Eventually, the tide turned in Garfield's favor. "I now know of none who does not say my vindication is complete," Garfield said with satisfaction. When Congress reconvened that winter, the salary increase was repealed.

THE DEGOLYER PAVEMENT SCANDAL

There was one more matter Garfield still had to face before his crucial campaign for re-election in 1874. It was the DeGolyer pavement scandal.

Early in the 1870s, the city of Washington had been reorganized and given a measure of home rule. The first task of the new Board of Public Works was to pave the capital's dirt roads. Many paving contractors competed for a share of the profitable job. Among them was the DeGolyer McClelland Company of Chicago. They were willing to pay up to $90,000 in "fees" to men who could help them get what ultimately amounted to a $700,000 contract.

In 1874 it was discovered that James A. Garfield had received $5,000 of that money. Garfield explained that the DeGolyer Company had hired Congressman Richard C. Parsons, an attorney from Ohio, to present their case before the Board of Public Works. Parsons had to leave town and asked

Garfield to take over for him while he was gone, which Garfield did. Afterward, when Parsons received his $16,000 fee, he paid $5,000 of it to Garfield for his services. It was nothing more than a legal fee, said Garfield.

The explanation would have satisfied everyone if an investigation had not revealed that the DeGolyer Company had distributed $72,000 more among others who had influence with the members of Washington's Board of Public Works. Many newspapers accused Garfield of selling his influence as chairman of the House Appropriations Committee. This time, without a moment's hesitation, Garfield rushed to his own defense.

THE ELECTION OF 1874

Although there had been moments in the last few years that James Garfield was not proud of, he was not worried in 1874 when election time rolled around. For six terms he had served in a "sure" district. He was so certain of being re-elected that he did not even plan to campaign. In fact, he was toying with the idea of going to Europe that summer. Then, in the spring, Harmon Austin told Garfield the bad news. People of the Western Reserve were seriously questioning his honesty and integrity. He would have to stay home and fight for his congressional seat.

Garfield won the Republican nomination, receiving 100 votes out of 134 cast at the district convention. But actually winning the election was a different story. The country was in the midst of a depression that was to last for five more years. Voters blamed the Republicans, the party in power, for the hard times. Garfield was criticized for every scandal he was ever a part of, including incidents dating back to the Civil War.

Garfield's most difficult job was to convince the voters that he was an honest man. Evidently he did, because in November 1874 the people of the 19th Congressional District of Ohio returned James Garfield to Congress. His total of 12,591 votes was down from the more than 19,000 he received in 1872, but Garfield was satisfied. To him his election was a moral victory—"the triumph of truth over error."

After the Election

The day after Christmas, Crete gave birth to another baby boy, making six children in all. He was named Edward (Neddie). Soon after, Garfield was off to the final session of the 43rd Congress, his last as chairman of the Appropriations Committee. When the session was over, Garfield took a trip to California, which he had put off for years.

Crete stayed home to care for the new baby and the rest of the children. Harry was now 11, Jimmy nine, Mollie, the only girl, was eight, and the two younger boys, Irvin and Abram, were five and two, respectively. Always the teacher, Garfield had the children follow his progress on a map and made each letter home a lesson in history or geography.

THE 44TH CONGRESS

Garfield returned to a Congress that was to be controlled by Democrats for the rest of his congressional career. He was now one of the senior Republican members in the House. No longer chairman of the Appropriations Committee, he was appointed to the Ways and Means and Pacific Railroad committees. The next year, when James G. Blaine was elected to the U.S. Senate, Garfield became Republican minority leader in the House.

In the winter of 1876, a Democratic bill was introduced giving long-delayed amnesty to a small group of southerners who were still barred from public service. Blaine immediately moved to exclude Jefferson Davis, not because he was the former president of the Confederacy, but on the grounds that he had been personally responsible for the horrors in the Confederate prison camp at Andersonville, Georgia. In an atmosphere charged with electricity, Garfield gave a passionate speech supporting Blaine's far-fetched statements about the mistreatment of Union soldiers at Andersonville. The speech opened all the old wounds that divided the country. Both Blaine and Garfield had also done their best to take the public's mind off the scandals of the Grant administration.

A New Ohio Home

Although the Garfields were well established in Washington, the sale of their house in Hiram had left them without a home in the Reserve. So in 1876, Garfield bought a small house and 160 acres of farmland at Mentor, Ohio. A highway ran past the front porch of the frame building and a railroad cut across a corner of the property. Garfield remodeled the house and built a cottage behind it which served as his library. When the house was enlarged to three floors, with a separate wing for Garfield's mother, the newspapers dubbed the farm "Lawnfield."

Chapter 9

The Dark Horse Candidate

I n 1876, despite the scandals in his administration, many Republicans urged Grant to run for a third term. When Grant declined, Garfield supported Maine Senator James G. Blaine's bid for the nomination. Governor Rutherford B. Hayes of Ohio was also gaining ground as a Republican candidate.

At the 1876 Republican National Convention, Blaine led for six ballots. Suddenly the tide turned, and Hayes won the nomination. Garfield was disappointed, but in the interest of party unity, he pledged his support to Hayes. The Democratic candidate was Samuel J. Tilden of New York.

Garfield was re-elected to his seat in the House, but sad news from home kept him from celebrating his victory. His son, Edward, was very ill with whooping cough. Shortly after Garfield returned to Ohio, Edward died. Once again, with sorrow in their hearts, the Garfields buried a child.

A DISPUTED ELECTION

As if Edward's death were not enough to cause Garfield unhappiness, the Republicans were in deep trouble. In the presidential election, Democrat Tilden had received 250,000 more popular votes than Hayes. Most people, including Garfield, thought Tilden had been elected. But Republican officials would not concede defeat until the votes of the electoral college were counted (presidential electors selected by the people of each state).

After doing some quick arithmetic, Republican leaders figured that Hayes still had a chance to be President. But they would have to prove vote fraud in several states that Tilden had carried. So they demanded a recount of the votes in South Carolina, Louisiana, and Florida, southern states that had Republican governments. President Grant chose Garfield to be part of a congressional committee that was to oversee the recount.

Garfield found that both sides had cheated. Republicans had voted repeatedly; Democrats had intimidated blacks to keep them from voting. But there was no doubt that Tilden had won. Garfield and the other Republicans on the recount committee got around that fact by arguing that more blacks would have voted Republican if they had not been afraid to go to the polls.

When the committee returned to Washington, the three southern states plus Oregon (another state in dispute) announced they were going to file two separate returns. This had never happened before. Garfield argued that the proper procedure was to give the presiding officer of the Senate full power to count the electoral votes while the rest of Congress watched. Because the president of the Senate was a Republican, Democrats would not hear of it. They insisted that the entire Congress—both the House and the Senate—where the Democrats were in the majority, had the final authority. In the end, a 15-member electoral commission, of which Garfield was a member, was appointed to decide between Hayes and Tilden.

A Compromise Settlement

For more than two weeks, the electoral commission argued back and forth. When they voted, it was strictly along party lines. Because the 15th member voted with the Republicans, Rutherford B. Hayes was named President. The Democrats were furious. They threatened to filibuster (make prolonged speeches) and delay Hayes' inauguration.

The threat forced the Republicans to come to an "understanding" with the Democrats. In return for stopping the filibuster, they promised that Hayes would remove all federal troops remaining in the South. They also agreed to respect the rights of blacks and to vote for federal funds for improvements in southern states.

Garfield, who hated political deals, played a key role in assuring the Democrats that the new administration would carry out the Republican promises. But he was careful not to make specific commitments. On March 4, 1877, Rutherford B. Hayes was inaugurated as the 19th President of the United States.

THE HAYES ADMINISTRATION

As promised, when Hayes took office, he withdrew the last of the federal troops from the South. Then the President turned to civil service reform. He appointed a commission to investigate abuses in the New York Customs House. An experienced politician, Hayes selected New York because New York Senator Roscoe Conkling, the leader of a Republican group known as the Stalwarts, had supporters who held jobs there. And Conkling was obstructing the administration's programs.

After a two-month investigation, Hayes' commission

reported widespread bribery and corruption in the Customs House. Hayes then fired Chester A. Arthur, the Customs Collector. Calling an emergency meeting of New York Republicans, Conkling quickly turned it into an antiadministration rally. Garfield warned the President to move more slowly with civil service reform in the interest of party unity.

A Needed Ally

The Democrats controlled the House, and the Republicans controlled the Senate. Garfield would have liked to be a senator, but Hayes persuaded him to remain in the House. The President said he needed an ally there to help him get his programs through. Garfield stayed in the House and did a good job for Hayes. He became one of the most effective Republican speakers and legislators in the House of Representatives.

Garfield was now in his late forties with thinning hair and a touch of gray in his beard. He had put in many long hours of hard work in the House and was ready for a change. Friends urged him to run for governor of Ohio. But that post did not interest him. Once again he had his eye on the U.S. Senate.

Senator-Elect Garfield

When Hayes announced early in his term that he would not seek re-election, a Garfield-for-President boom was started by friends in Wisconsin and Pennsylvania. Garfield asked his managers to lobby instead for the post of senator on his behalf. But privately he kept in touch with the supporters who wanted him to run for President.

The Ohio legislature met on January 6, 1880, to select a U.S. senator. With the support of John Sherman, Garfield was nominated and approved as the next senator from Ohio by unanimous vote. He had finally achieved his ambition! Upon being congratulated by a friend, Garfield was so joyful that he gave the man a bear hug. Then, lifting his friend off his feet, Garfield swung him around in circles.

Senator-elect Garfield claimed he had gained his office without making any deals. It was not exactly true. His managers had traded chairmanships and other offices in return for support of Garfield in the Senate race. Moreover, Garfield was committed to Sherman for President.

THE REPUBLICAN CONVENTION OF 1880

Before the Republican National Convention of 1880 even opened in Chicago, there was a struggle for power. Roscoe Conkling had persuaded former President Grant to run for the presidency again. Never before had a President who had served two terms and retired wanted to run again. The other major candidates for the Republican nomination were James G. Blaine and John Sherman, whom Garfield was pledged to support. The Republicans were split into two factions: Conkling's group (the Stalwarts) and Blaine's group (the Half-Breeds), accused by Conkling of being half-hearted party members.

Sherman's Chances

John Sherman had a good chance of capturing the Republican nomination for President as a compromise candidate if Grant or Blaine could not get enough votes to win. The two front runners had many friends, but they also had many enemies.

But was Sherman the best choice for a compromise candidate? As secretary of the treasury in the Hayes Cabinet, he had made reform-minded Republicans angry by giving out patronage jobs (those awarded for political support) in Louisiana, Florida, and South Carolina after the presidential vote recount. He had also angered those who were against reform by advising President Rutherford B. Hayes to fire Chester A. Arthur, the Customs Collector in New York City. So Sherman had enemies, too. Maybe what the Republicans needed was a good dark horse candidate (a little known contestant).

Sherman asked Garfield to attend the convention and place his name in nomination. Garfield had not planned to go to Chicago. He had supported Sherman only to unite the Ohio delegation against Grant. Now he was suddenly chief spokesman for a man he was not even fond of. But Garfield had promised Sherman his support, and he would not let Sherman down.

Garfield Support Grows

Arriving in Chicago a week early, Garfield spent most of his time talking against a third term for Grant. The convention opened on June 2 with over 15,000 delegates and spectators present. It was held in an immense auditorium that was as wide as a city block and twice as long. Every time Garfield entered the noisy, crowded hall, he was greeted by cheers from the galleries. Wharton Barker, a Philadelphia banker who supported Garfield, had planned it. Whenever Garfield's name was mentioned, Barker's men cheered loudly. Sometimes others joined them who did not want Grant or Blaine.

By June 4 Garfield suspected that he could be the Republican's dark horse candidate. "The signs are multiplying," he wrote to Crete in Ohio, "that the convention is strongly turning its attention to me." But because he was committed to John Sherman, Garfield would not give his backers permission to

In 1880, the fight for the Republican presidential nomination was between Ulysses S. Grant and James G. Blaine. After 33 ballots, neither man had won. On the 34th ballot, Wisconsin announced its votes for Garfield. He had not even been nominated! But Garfield became the Republicans' unanimous choice on the 38th ballot. For Vice-President, the delegates chose Chester A. Arthur. (Library of Congress.)

nominate him. As usual, Garfield's friends understood him. They would bring up his name when the time was right.

A Deadlocked Convention

Nominations began on the night of June 5. Blaine first, then Grant. Garfield followed Conkling's dramatic nomination of Grant with a low-key speech for party unity. After describing the qualities needed by the next President, he asked, "What do we want?" A voice from the gallery shouted, "We want Garfield!" Ignoring the interruption, Garfield worked his way around to nominating Sherman. Everyone but Sherman's supporters thought it was a good speech.

The convention struggled to nominate a candidate. On the first ballot, Grant led with 304 votes. On the second, one of Barker's men cast a vote for Garfield. Garfield would not allow his name to be put into nomination, but Barker had cleverly reminded the convention delegates that there was now a possible compromise candidate in the hall. The voting continued. And after 28 ballots, the convention adjourned, still deadlocked.

The next day, Sherman gained a few votes, but nothing changed. Then, on the 34th ballot, in a surprise move, the Wisconsin delegation switched their votes to James A. Garfield. The hall suddenly grew quiet. Garfield had not even been nominated! He struggled to his feet and pointed that out. The weary chairman ordered Garfield to sit down. Everyone was too anxious to nominate a candidate to worry about rules of order. On the next ballot, the 35th, Indiana got into line behind Wisconsin. Garfield's total was now 50 votes.

A Surprise Nominee

Excitement filled the hall as the 36th ballot began. Grant supporters stood firm. The ex-President still had 306 votes. But all of Grant's enemies had now rallied around James Garfield, who received 399 votes. This was more than enough to be the Republican nominee for President.

Garfield's nomination had certainly come as a surprise. But the convention's choice of Chester A. Arthur as his Vice-President was even more of a surprise. Arthur was a Grant Stalwart and one of Roscoe Conkling's chief lieutenants. The Democrats passed over Tilden, the nominal head of the Democratic Party during the Hayes administration. And they, too, nominated a dark horse. He was General Winfield Scott Hancock of Pennsylvania.

THE FRONT PORCH CAMPAIGN

Garfield went home to Ohio to conduct a "front porch" campaign. In 1880 presidential hopefuls did not campaign for themselves. Instead, their supporters made speeches on their behalf. Garfield was told to "sit cross-legged and look wise until after the election." Mentor had never known such excitement. Trainloads of people, from school children to senators, came to shake Garfield's hand. And each day he received at least 100 pieces of mail.

By late July, all signs pointed to a close election. The South was sure to go Democratic. And although the Republicans seemed to have the edge in the East and Midwest, it was by a much narrower margin. Garfield knew he would be defeated unless he was able to heal the wounds within the Republican Party. Blaine and Sherman were still smarting from their defeats, but it was Conkling and the New York Stalwarts who refused to campaign for the ticket.

Mending Fences

Garfield's advisors suggested that he go to New York and make peace with Roscoe Conkling. In the hope of gaining party unity, Garfield agreed to go. He left for New York on August 3. During the two-day trip, he made more than 20 rear-platform train appearances. His oratory was spellbinding, and at every stop, the crowds grew larger. Garfield arrived in New York City full of confidence.

On the evening of his arrival, Garfield held a meeting with some of the city's wealthiest men. Garfield told them that victory was doubtful without their generous support. Levi P. Morton, an important financier, agreed to become finance chairman of the Republican National Committee. By the time the meeting ended, the business community was solidly behind Garfield.

Almost every prominent Republican was at a meeting at the Fifth Avenue Hotel the next day, including Sherman and Blaine. Both men were cordial to Garfield. Roscoe Conkling, however, had purposely left town. He sent a message to Garfield to come to his Coney Island retreat.

Garfield's patience was worn thin. He would not go one step farther to talk to Conkling. Instead, Garfield dealt with Conkling's lieutenants. It proved to be a wise move. The Conkling men promised Garfield the full support of the New York organization. In return, Garfield told the Stalwarts that he would remember them when it was time to distribute patronage jobs.

Garfield went home well satisfied. He had accomplished his objectives without making any deals. At least nothing had been spelled out in detail to anyone. However, those who attended the meetings thought that definite promises had indeed been made. Many seeds of misunderstanding were sown at the meetings in New York.

The high point of Garfield's front porch campaign was when Conkling, Grant, and some friends dropped in at Lawnfield after a meeting. Conkling was then speaking at rallies around the country and working for the Republican ticket—but not for Garfield. Nevertheless, the candidate for President was relieved that party fences had been mended, at least officially.

The Morey Letter

From the moment he was nominated in June, the Democrats accused Garfield of corruption in the government scandals of 1873. Then in September, the campaign heated up even more. Democrats painted the number 329, the money allegedly paid to Garfield by the Credit Mobilier, on sidewalks, fences, and even on the steps of Garfield's Washington home.

But in the final weeks of the campaign, the Democrats went one step too far in campaign trickery. On October 20, a New York City scandal sheet named *Truth* printed a letter that supposedly was written by James Garfield to H. L. Morey of the Employers Union of Lynn, Massachusetts. The letter said that Garfield favored the importation of cheap Chinese labor to compete with American workers. It caused a sensation.

Garfield immediately denounced the Morey letter as a forgery. And although it later proved to be a fake, the Democrats continued to use the item to hurt Garfield's campaign. The forgery may have caused Garfield to lose the states of Nevada and California. Both the Democrats and *Truth* later apologized to Garfield for using the letter to discredit him.

VICTORY

Election day, November 2, 1880, dawned clear and sunny. After supervising the fall planting, Garfield walked to the Town Hall to vote. Then he returned home to await the results. By 11 o'clock that night, Garfield knew that he had carried New York, a key state. Shortly after midnight he sat down to supper with about 25 friends. Not long after, Garfield was informed that he was President-elect of the United States.

It was a close but decisive election. Although Garfield

The presidential election of 1880 was based mostly on personalities, not issues. Buttons, posters, and songs kept the campaign lively. This poster portrays Garfield as an honest, patriotic farmer who is hacking away at evils such as fraud, hatred, and falsehood on his way to the White House. (Library of Congress.)

had won by only 7,368 popular votes, he had 214 electoral votes to Hancock's 155. Garfield considered it a personal triumph. Yet, he said, "I am sad because I am about to say goodbye to a long series of happy years which I fear terminate with 1880."

Chapter 10

Assuming the Presidency

Although James Garfield was elected President in November 1880, he did not take office until March 1881. Soon after the election, he resigned from the U.S. House of Representatives. Then he resigned from the post that he had never filled – that of U.S. senator from the state of Ohio.

During the winter, Garfield had two important jobs to do – appoint his Cabinet and write his inaugural speech. He told a friend that he was going to move as slowly as Lincoln. "I want to take a bath in public opinion," he said.

Every day the President-elect and his two secretaries were deluged with mail. The majority of the letters either contained advice or asked for favors. Garfield was also plagued by long lines of office seekers who descended on Lawnfield.

In late November, the Garfields went to Washington. The President-elect conferred with various politicians while Crete supervised the packing of their belongings and the closing of their Washington house. Then it was back to Lawnfield, where Garfield settled down to select his Cabinet.

Soldier, scholar, and statesman, James Abram Garfield devoted his life to public service. Garfield had served only 200 days as President when he died from a wound inflicted by a disappointed office seeker. His death brought pressure for civil service reform. (Library of Congress.)

CABINET APPOINTMENTS

There were seven Cabinet positions to fill. As a compromise candidate, Garfield knew all factions of the party and each section of the country had to be represented. Advice poured in from every prominent Republican who had helped him get elected. He did not know whom to trust. Everyone seemed to want something.

James G. Blaine headed Garfield's list for secretary of state. He liked Blaine and owed him a debt for his support in Chicago. Giving Blaine the Cabinet post with the most prestige would also satisfy the New Englanders. It was a perfect choice, except that Garfield worried that Blaine might run for President in 1884. Garfield put the question to Blaine, "If I should ask you to take a place in the Cabinet, what would be your probable response, and before you answer, please tell me whether you are, or will be, a candidate for the presidency in 1884. . . . " Blaine replied that he would never again run for the presidency.

No doubt, Blaine meant it. As it turned out, however, he was a presidential candidate every four years for the rest of his life. Believing that Blaine was not a threat to a second term, Garfield offered him the post of secretary of state. Blaine accepted just before Christmas.

The Stalwarts were angry when news of Blaine's appointment leaked out. Conkling demanded to name the secretary of the treasury, which was the second most important Cabinet post. In addition to power over currency and the tariff, the secretary of the treasury was in charge of the New York customs house, which controlled 1,500 jobs.

The Fight Over Treasury

Conkling asked the President to appoint Levi P. Morton, financial chairman of Garfield's presidential campaign, to be secretary of the treasury. Garfield refused; it was illegal for a banker to hold a high treasury post. Besides, westerners would be furious if the Treasury Department were handed to a Wall Street banker. Conkling sent his men to Lawnfield to remind Garfield that he had promised the treasury position to Morton at their meeting in New York. Garfield denied making any such definite commitments.

When Sherman's men heard that Conkling wanted the treasury for Morton, they pressured the President-elect to retain Sherman in the post. Garfield was indebted to Sherman for his help in the Senate election, but he did not want him in his Cabinet. When they discussed the matter, Sherman said he would prefer the Senate seat Garfield had just vacated to a Cabinet post. Garfield used his influence with the Ohio legislature, and Sherman was elected senator.

That did not solve the treasury appointment, though. To appease the Stalwarts, Garfield suggested giving a different Cabinet post to a New Yorker. The Stalwarts said it had to be the treasury position or Conkling would make trouble for Garfield in Congress. Garfield invited Conkling to a face-to-face meeting in Mentor, where, on February 16, 1881, the two men spent more than eight hours discussing the Cabinet. But Conkling did not budge about the treasury post, and neither did Garfield. Ten days later, Garfield, in a bold move, offered Levi Morton the post of secretary of the Navy, and he accepted.

Other Cabinet Selections

Because Garfield was to leave for Washington on February 28, he hurried to complete his Cabinet selections. Robert Todd Lincoln, son of Abraham Lincoln, accepted the War Department with thanks. His appointment satisfied the Stalwarts of the West—particularly Illinois. Minnesota Senator William Windom was Garfield's choice for secretary of the treasury.

But Blaine persuaded the President to wait before extending a firm offer. Wayne MacVeagh of Pennsylvania was named attorney general. For secretary of the interior, Garfield's choice was Senator William Boyd Allison of Iowa, but Allison declined. Judge William H. Hunt of Louisiana was tentatively slated for postmaster general.

On the last day of February, with his Cabinet fairly well settled, James Garfield and his family left Mentor for Washington. But when the President arrived at the nation's capital, he found that the Cabinet was not settled after all. Blaine convinced the President-elect to appoint Allison secretary of the treasury instead of Windom. Garfield then withdrew his offer to Windom and sent feelers to Allison. While Blaine worked to put his friends into the Cabinet, Conkling was doing just the opposite. He had put pressure on Morton not to accept the Navy post. And with the inauguration only 48 hours away, Morton withdrew.

Garfield then did something that brought him in open conflict with Conkling. Without consulting the Stalwart leader, he selected Thomas L. James, a Conkling supporter, to be postmaster general instead of Hunt. As the former postmaster of New York City, James was a good choice for the job. But for Garfield to appoint a man from Conkling's machine without the approval of its leader was unheard of. When James accepted the post, Conkling lashed out at Garfield for being a traitor to his party. Nevertheless, Garfield did not back down.

THE INAUGURATION

On inauguration day, March 4, 1881, Garfield awoke to a cold, blustery morning. Within the hour, Senator Allison arrived and told him he could not accept the post of secretary of the treasury. Realizing then that Allison and Conkling were allies, Garfield could see a showdown coming. The big question was: Would the Republican Party be controlled from the White House or from the Congress? The answer to that question had to wait. It was 10:30, and President Hayes' carriage had arrived to take the President-elect to the White House. From there, accompanied by a committee of senators, Garfield went to the Capitol.

In the Senate gallery sat Crete, the children, and Garfield's mother, Eliza. They watched as Chester A. Arthur was sworn in as Vice-President. Then everyone went outdoors to the East Portico. Crete was proud of her husband—the tall, balding, bearded man who was seated in the chair once occupied by George Washington.

The Inaugural Address

Garfield's inaugural address was forthright and optimistic. He began by saying, "We stand today upon an eminence which overlooks a hundred years of national life—a century crowded with perils, but crowned with the triumphs of liberty and law. . . . " The highlight of Garfield's address was when he noted that the elevation of the blacks from slavery to citizenship was the "most important political change . . . since the adoption of the Constitution." He vowed to protect the blacks' newly won rights, especially the right to vote. After promising to keep close tabs on government spending, he concluded by saying that civil service must be regulated by law.

When the address ended, Garfield was sworn in by Morrison Waite, Chief Justice of the Supreme Court. Then James Abram Garfield, 20th President of the United States, bent down to kiss his mother. Eighty-year-old Eliza was beaming. She always knew her son was destined for greatness. Mrs. Garfield was the first mother of a President in American history to attend her son's inauguration.

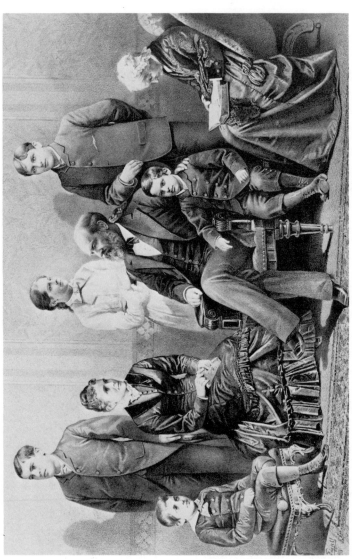

President Garfield and his family in 1881. Seated from left to right: Abram (Little Abe), Lucretia (Crete), the President, Irvin McDowell, and the President's mother, Eliza. Standing from left to right: James Rudolph (Jim), Mollie, and Harry Augustus (Hal). (Library of Congress.)

After luncheon with the Hayes, there was a parade, an evening reception, and a ball in the new National Museum (the Smithsonian Institution). It was 11 o'clock when Garfield and his wife returned to the White House. At the President's request, Senator Windom was there. Garfield offered Windom the post of secretary of the treasury, and he accepted. Hunt had been moved over to the Navy to replace Morton, and Iowa Senator Samuel J. Kirkwood was named secretary of the interior. Garfield's Cabinet was finally complete. He sent his nominations to the Senate, now in special session. All the men were unanimously confirmed.

THE NEW ADMINISTRATION

The entire Garfield family now lived in the White House, including Eliza. It was a drafty old mansion of 31 rooms with worn furnishings and threadbare carpet. Yet it was alive with history, and First Lady Crete seemed to blossom there.

The new President hired Joseph Stanley Brown, a young campaign worker from Mentor, to be his private secretary. Joe and Mollie, the President's daughter, fell in love. Several years later, after Crete sent Joe to college, he and Mollie were married at Lawnfield. In 1881 Joe presided over a small staff that handled the President's correspondence and arranged his appointments.

The Spoils System at Work

Over 100,000 civilians were employed by the federal government, and the President had to make all the appointments. The hordes of office seekers who filed through the oval office were the torment of Garfield's day. Although he hated squabbling over jobs, Garfield had no quarrels with the spoils system. His appointments read like a list of his Hiram friends and army buddies. But he could see the need for civil service reform, not from a moral standpoint, but because the government was getting too big for one person to make all appointments.

President Garfield had promised Republican leaders that he would consult with them before making political appointments in their states. Starting with New York on March 20, 1881, he asked Senators Conkling and Platt for their advice. Platt was out of town, so Garfield met alone with Roscoe Conkling at the White House. After a long discussion, Garfield agreed to most of Conkling's suggestions, which involved appointments of Stalwarts. But when it came to rewarding independent Republicans who had campaigned for Garfield, Conkling told the President to assign them to foreign countries.

Having Second Thoughts

Garfield sent the names of nine Stalwarts to the Senate for confirmation. Because independent Republicans had received no recognition, it was thought that Garfield was controlled by Conkling. When James Blaine pointed this out to him, Garfield began having second thoughts. He told Crete, "I have broken Blaine's heart . . . I have acted too hastily."

Suddenly, without any explanations, Garfield sent the Senate a new list of names for the very same appointments. One of those on Garfield's new list was Judge William H. Robertson, a leader of the New York Independent Republicans and an enemy of Senator Conkling's. Garfield chose Robertson to be collector of customs at New York City. The incumbent collector, Edwin A. Merritt, was named consul general in London.

Conkling was outraged at Garfield's about-face. Robertson's appointment struck at the very base of Conkling's power.

The President knew he would have a fight on his hands. But it was going to be worse than he had imagined.

THE SHOWDOWN

Several members of the Cabinet threatened to resign. Quickly, the President and Postmaster General James devised a compromise. Merritt would be retained for the time being as collector of customs, and Robertson would be named district attorney. All that was needed was Conkling's blessing to end the crisis. But Conkling did not show up at the White House for the compromise meeting. The President was fuming. It was time for a showdown.

Blaine egged Garfield on. He and his supporters wanted to destroy Conkling's political power. But with Garfield it was a fight for principle. He had been on the other side of the fence during President Andrew Johnson's quarrel with Congress. Now that he was President, he said, "This brings on the contest at once and will settle the question whether the President is registering clerk of the Senate or the executive of the United States."

Breaking the Deadlock

There were 37 Republicans in the Senate and 37 Democrats. There were also two independents, one of whom was pledged to vote with the Democrats. General William Mahone of Virginia was the other. Having the decisive vote, Mahone traded his cooperation with the Republicans for several choice committee posts. Because the Democrats protested Mahone's actions by filibustering, the Senate could not act on Garfield's controversial appointments.

On May 4 the southern Democrats broke the deadlock, ending the filibuster. Withdrawing five New York nominations of Conkling's friends, Garfield forced the Senate to act on the Robertson nomination. The Stalwarts knew they had lost the fight. And on May 17, 1881, Senators Conkling and Platt resigned their Senate seats. The new customs collector was confirmed on the following day.

On the same day that the Senate's filibuster was broken, Crete fell ill with malaria. The President spent hours at her bedside nursing her back to health.

Other Actions and Activities

Soon after he took office, President Garfield asked Postmaster General James to investigate corruption in the post office. In sparsely populated areas where mail could not be delivered by rail or ship, contracts were given out for these routes to be serviced by other means with "certainty, celerity and security" (postal workers used asterisks or stars for the words, thus the name "Star Routes"). When James reported widespread fraud, Garfield asked Assistant Postmaster Thomas Brady, who was in charge of the Star Routes, and others involved in the scandal, to resign. It saved the government millions of dollars each year.

In foreign affairs, the foundation was laid for a strong U.S. policy in Latin America. And in the Pacific, Garfield recognized the importance of the Sandwich Islands (now Hawaii) to American trade interests.

As summer began, Garfield looked forward to a vacation. He was to leave on July 2 with sons Harry and Jim for Williams College. There he would attend his 25th class reunion and enroll the boys in the freshman class. He planned to pick up Crete and the other children at a seaside resort in Elberon, New Jersey, where Crete was recuperating from her bout with malaria.

The night before he left, Garfield went to visit Blaine. He did not notice the short, bearded man, who was following him, clutching an ivory-handled revolver inside his pocket. It was Charles Guiteau.

Biography of an Assassin

Charles Julius Guiteau was born in Illinois of French Huguenot ancestry. After his mother died when he was seven, he was raised by his father, Luther, in Freeport, Illinois. As a young man he joined the Oneida Community, a religious cult in upper New York state. After five years, Guiteau left for New York City, where he planned to start a religious paper. It did not work out, so he studied law at the office of George Scoville, his sister's husband. He was admitted to the Illinois bar after a short and not very thorough examination.

Guiteau then married Annie Bunn, a librarian at a social service organization. Life with Guiteau proved miserable for Annie. Because he was often cruel to her, she divorced him after five years of marriage.

Failing as a trial lawyer, Guiteau started a collection business. But in 1874 he lost his collection business and was thrown into jail for stealing his clients' money. His brother-in-law bailed him out and took him to Wisconsin to live. Guiteau's sister was sympathetic toward him until he went after her with an axe. A local doctor agreed that he was mentally ill and should be put in an institution. But before anything could be done, Guiteau ran away to Chicago and became a religious lecturer.

In 1880 Guiteau's interest turned to politics. Always scheming, he took an old speech and converted it into one for Grant. When Garfield was nominated instead of Grant, Guiteau printed the speech in a pamphlet and changed the title to "Garfield Against Hancock." Although the speech was never delivered, Guiteau thought he was responsible for Garfield's victory and expected to be rewarded with a government post.

Arriving in Washington, Guiteau was one of the hordes of office seekers who plagued President Garfield daily. Finally, he was told to see the secretary of state. At the state department, Guiteau managed to talk to Secretary of State James G. Blaine several times. On May 14, 1881, Blaine lost patience with Guiteau and told him that there was "no prospect whatever" of his being appointed minister to Paris. Guiteau was devastated.

Reading about the resignations of Conkling and Platt on May 16, Guiteau blamed Garfield for causing trouble for him and the Republican Party. If only Garfield were out of the way and Arthur was President, all would be well. The thought preyed on Guiteau's twisted mind. By the beginning of June he was convinced that he was chosen by God to "remove" President Garfield.

On June 8, with 10 dollars he had borrowed from an acquaintance, Guiteau bought an ivory-handled revolver. Then, for over a month, Guiteau followed Garfield wherever he went. With the gun in his pocket, he waited for the right moment to pull the trigger.

After James Garfield died, Charles Guiteau was tried for murder. His lawyers wanted him to plead insanity, but he would not. Guiteau was convinced until the end that the Lord had

*Charles J. Guiteau was a disappointed office seeker who shot
President Garfield because he thought the Lord had chosen him
to "rid the country of a traitor" and make the Stalwart, Chester
Arthur, President. He was executed in 1882.* (Library of
Congress.)

chosen him to kill the President. The jury
found him guilty. On June 30, 1882, before a
huge crowd at the District of Columbia jail,
Charles Julius Guiteau was hanged for the
murder of James A. Garfield, the 20th President of the United States.

Chapter 11

The Killing of
the President

On Friday, July 1, 1881, the newspapers announced that President Garfield would leave the next day for Elberon. Several Cabinet members and their wives were joining him. Charles Guiteau had been stalking the President for over a month. Convinced that he was chosen by God to kill Garfield, he was waiting for the opportune moment. Garfield's trip presented just such a moment.

THE SHOOTING

Guiteau arrived at the Baltimore and Potomac Railroad Station in Washington early the next morning. As President Garfield and Secretary Blaine walked through the ladies' waiting room, he came up behind the President and fired two shots. Several Cabinet members heard the shots and rushed into the waiting room. They found Secretary Blaine kneeling over the President, who was lying in a faint on the floor.

Harry and Jim, who had come in another carriage, raced to their father's side. When the President regained consciousness, he was carried upstairs to a large empty room to await the doctors' arrival. And word was sent to Crete that her husband had been wounded.

Although several physicians examined the wounded President at the depot, they could not locate the bullet still in his body. Later, when Garfield insisted on going home, mattresses were ripped from a Pullman railroad car and piled in a wagon. Carefully, the President was placed in the improvised ambulance. A crowd followed the horses all the way to the White House.

Guiteau's Letter

Charles Guiteau was captured immediately after the shooting and taken to jail. Proclaiming proudly, "I am a Stalwart. Arthur is now President!" he gave the officers this note.

> To the White House: July 2, 1881
>   The President's tragic death was a sad necessity; but it will unite the Republican party and save the Republic. Life is a flimsy dream, and it matters little when one goes. A human life is of small value. During the war thousands of brave boys went down without a tear. I presume that the President was a Christian, and that he will be happier in Paradise than here. It will be no worse for Mrs. Garfield, dear soul, to part with her husband this way than by natural death. He is liable to go at any time anyway. I had no ill will toward the President. His death was a political necessity. I am a lawyer, a theologian and a politician. I am a Stalwart of the Stalwarts. . . . I am going to the jail.

Guiteau also had written a letter to General William T. Sherman. In it he asked Sherman to rush troops to the jail in the event of a lynching (hanging) attempt by enraged citizens. He stood trial, however, and was later hanged for his crime.

THE PRESIDENT'S WOUND

Although Garfield had been hit by both bullets fired by Guiteau, he was not dead. Doctors who examined him found that the first bullet had gone through his left shoulder and passed out of his body. The second had entered the right side of his back. That one had stayed inside his body. It struck the eleventh rib on the right side and passed in front of the spinal cord without severing it.

Although the second bullet drove a number of pieces of bone into the surrounding tissue, it stopped just below the pancreas. Considering the size of the bullet and the kind of wound it was, it had actually done very little damage. The wound would not be thought of as serious today. At that time though, doctors were sure the bullet had punctured a vital organ. When the President asked what his chances of survival were, a doctor in attendance answered, "One in a hundred."

The Wound Becomes Infected

Crete arrived the night of the shooting prepared for the worst. She was relieved to find the President still alive and in good spirits. The next morning, specialists were called in from New York and Philadelphia. Although they were unable to find the bullet, they could tell that it had not struck a vital organ. At that time, there were no X-ray machines. However, Alexander Graham Bell, inventor of the telephone, was brought in to look for the bullet with an electrical metal detector that he had invented. But the results were inconclusive because of interference from the metal bedsprings. So many dirty fingers and instruments poked at Garfield's wound that it be-

Doctors attending Garfield after he had been wounded. Be-
cause of constant probing with dirty fingers and instruments to
find the bullet still lodged in the President's body, the wound
became infected. The President died at Elberon, New Jersey,
on September 19, 1881, at 10:35 P.M. (Library of Congress.)

came infected. Without antibiotics, there was no way to stop
the infection.

During July, August, and early September, the government ran itself as its chief executive lay in bed fighting for
his life. Health bulletins were issued three times a day. Con-
gregations in every church in the country prayed for the Presi-

dent's recovery. Get-well telegrams poured in from all over the world. Wounded and helpless, patiently enduring the pain day after day, Garfield became a hero to the public.

However, all the probing and pushing by the doctors only made the infection worse. In September, the President longed to get away from the terrible summer heat of the capital. The doctors moved Garfield to Elberon, where it was hoped that the cool sea air would help him recover.

DEATH OF THE PRESIDENT

After arriving at Elberon, Garfield became weaker. He now knew there was no hope for his recovery. On September 18, he asked his secretary, "Do you think my name will have a place in history?" "Yes," was the reply. "A grand one, but a grander place in human hearts." On the night of September 19, 1881 (the anniversary of the Battle of Chickamauga), at 10:35 P.M., President James Abram Garfield died.

His body lay in state in the Capitol rotunda for two days. It was a fitting tribute to Garfield, who had spent 17 years in the House of Representatives serving under the same rotunda. Over 70,000 people, including the new President, Chester A. Arthur, the Cabinet, and former Presidents Hayes and Grant, passed by his casket.

Following a service in Washington, a special train carried Garfield's body to Cleveland for the public funeral. It was held only blocks from the riverfront where he had been a canal boy. Almost the entire population of Cleveland paid their respects to the fallen President. Garfield's Mentor friends, the 42nd Ohio, and the Army of the Cumberland also were well represented.

After the service the President's body was laid to rest

in a vault in Lakeview Cemetery. In two months, James A. Garfield would have been 50 years old. Eliza outlived her son by seven years, and Crete lived in Mentor, devoted to her husband's memory, until her death in 1918.

GARFIELD'S LEGACY

As a state senator and U.S. congressman, Garfield had been involved in all the important issues in the nation for two decades. Because he was familiar with every facet of state and national government, Garfield may have been a great President if he had lived to serve out his term. But 200 days in office (80 of which he was wounded and in pain) were not long enough to show what kind of President he could be. However, although his tenure was brief, the office of President was stronger when he left it because of his showdown with the Senate over the right to make appointments.

What about James Garfield the private man? Born into poverty, he was a complicated intellectual who kept growing and changing. In his youth, he cherished female friendships and his personal freedom. But he became a strong family man who fell in love with his wife years after their wedding. Garfield was a pacifist turned soldier, a preacher turned teacher, an educator turned politician.

Although outgoing and friendly, Garfield was often filled with self-doubt. And he tended to sidestep problems by smoothing them over. Admitting that he was involved in the Credit Mobilier scandal and other dubious affairs, he gave misleading answers to questions about the roles he played. And he probably caused the trouble with Senator Conkling by misleading Levi Morton into thinking he promised him the position as secretary of the treasury.

A Fitting Memorial

Perhaps what Garfield will be remembered for most is civil service reform, for which he was indirectly responsible. Anger over his assassination brought about the passage of the Pendleton Bill on January 16, 1883. The bill established a bipartisan Civil Service Commission. Many government jobs were then placed under civil service and office seekers had to take competitive exams to qualify for them. Although a memorial tower was erected in memory of James Abram Garfield at Lakeview Cemetery, the Pendleton Bill is probably the most fitting memorial for the 20th President of the United States.

Bibliography

Feis, Ruth. *Mollie Garfield in the White House.* Chicago: Rand McNally, 1963. President Garfield was the author's grandfather, and Mollie was her mother. Feis has written a lovely family portrait gleaned from anecdotes from her mother and grandmother, and from various family diaries and letters.

Hoyt, Edwin P. *James A. Garfield.* Chicago: Reilly and Lee, 1964. A fact-filled biography for young people. It explores the years preceding Garfield's election to the presidency, during which he was one of the most powerful legislators in the United States.

Leech, Margaret, and Brown, Harry J. *The Garfield Orbit.* New York: Harper and Row, 1978. A well-researched, detailed, full-length adult biography about the life of President James A. Garfield, complete with notes and references. For good readers.

McElroy, Richard L. *James A. Garfield: His Life and Times.* Canton, Ohio: Daring Books, 1986. A fascinating history of James A. Garfield in pictures. He was the first President whose life could be documented through photographs. In these photos we also obtain a good look into America's past.

Taylor, John M. *Garfield of Ohio.* New York: W.W. Norton, 1970. A look at the complex personality of James A. Garfield through the pages of his diary. We see the conflict between Garfield's driving ambition and his desire for approval, which at times combined to make him seem indecisive.

Index

PRESIDENTS OF THE UNITED STATES

GEORGE WASHINGTON	L. Falkof	0-944483-19-4
JOHN ADAMS	R. Stefoff	0-944483-10-0
THOMAS JEFFERSON	R. Stefoff	0-944483-07-0
JAMES MADISON	B. Polikoff	0-944483-22-4
JAMES MONROE	R. Stefoff	0-944483-11-9
JOHN QUINCY ADAMS	M. Greenblatt	0-944483-21-6
ANDREW JACKSON	R. Stefoff	0-944483-08-9
MARTIN VAN BUREN	R. Ellis	0-944483-12-7
WILLIAM HENRY HARRISON	R. Stefoff	0-944483-54-2
JOHN TYLER	L. Falkof	0-944483-60-7
JAMES K. POLK	M. Greenblatt	0-944483-04-6
ZACHARY TAYLOR	D. Collins	0-944483-17-8
MILLARD FILLMORE	K. Law	0-944483-61-5
FRANKLIN PIERCE	F. Brown	0-944483-25-9
JAMES BUCHANAN	D. Collins	0-944483-62-3
ABRAHAM LINCOLN	R. Stefoff	0-944483-14-3
ANDREW JOHNSON	R. Stevens	0-944483-16-X
ULYSSES S. GRANT	L. Falkof	0-944483-02-X
RUTHERFORD B. HAYES	N. Robbins	0-944483-23-2
JAMES A. GARFIELD	F. Brown	0-944483-63-1
CHESTER A. ARTHUR	R. Stevens	0-944483-05-4
GROVER CLEVELAND	D. Collins	0-944483-01-1
BENJAMIN HARRISON	R. Stevens	0-944483-15-1
WILLIAM McKINLEY	D. Collins	0-944483-55-0
THEODORE ROOSEVELT	R. Stefoff	0-944483-09-7
WILLIAM H. TAFT	L. Falkof	0-944483-56-9
WOODROW WILSON	D. Collins	0-944483-18-6
WARREN G. HARDING	A. Canadeo	0-944483-64-X
CALVIN COOLIDGE	R. Stevens	0-944483-57-7

HERBERT C. HOOVER	B. Polikoff	0-944483-58-5
FRANKLIN D. ROOSEVELT	M. Greenblatt	0-944483-06-2
HARRY S. TRUMAN	D. Collins	0-944483-00-3
DWIGHT D. EISENHOWER	R. Ellis	0-944483-13-5
JOHN F. KENNEDY	L. Falkof	0-944483-03-8
LYNDON B. JOHNSON	L. Falkof	0-944483-20-8
RICHARD M. NIXON	R. Stefoff	0-944483-59-3
GERALD R. FORD	D. Collins	0-944483-65-8
JAMES E. CARTER	D. Richman	0-944483-24-0
RONALD W. REAGAN	N. Robbins	0-944483-66-6
GEORGE H.W. BUSH	R. Stefoff	0-944483-67-4

GARRETT EDUCATIONAL CORPORATION
130 EAST 13TH STREET
ADA, OK 74820